TRADING FOR GROWTH

POLICY ANALYSES IN INTERNATIONAL ECONOMICS 11

TRADING FOR GROWTH: THE NEXT ROUND OF TRADE NEGOTIATIONS

Gary Clyde Hufbauer
Jeffrey J. Schott

INSTITUTE FOR INTERNATIONAL ECONOMICS
WASHINGTON, DC
SEPTEMBER 1985

Gary Clyde Hufbauer was a Senior Fellow at the Institute for International Economics when he completed this analysis. He is now the Marcus Wallenberg Professor of International Financial Diplomacy at Georgetown University. Hufbauer was formerly Deputy Assistant Secretary for International Trade and Investment Policy of the US Treasury; Director of the International Tax Staff at the Treasury; and Professor of Economics at the University of New Mexico.

Jeffrey J. Schott is a Research Associate at the Institute. He was formerly a Senior Associate at the Carnegie Endowment for International Peace and an international economist at the US Treasury Department.

The authors are particularly grateful for detailed comments on earlier drafts by Bela Balassa, Robert Baldwin, C. Fred Bergsten, Richard N. Cooper, Joseph A. Greenwald, J. David Richardson, Leonard Weiss, and Alan Wm. Wolff. They derived many useful insights from discussions with members of an Institute study group composed of knowledgeable experts from business, government, and academia which met on December 13, 1984, and June 18, 1985, and offered frequent informal counsel throughout the study. G.C.H. and J.J.S.

Library of Congress Cataloging in Publication Data
Hufbauer, Gary Clyde.
Trading for growth.
(Policy analyses in international economics; 11)
"September 1985"
Includes bibliographical references.
1. International economic relations. 2. Commercial policy.
I. Schott, Jeffrey J., 1949-
II. Institute for International Economics (U.S.).
III. Title.
HF1411.H84   1985   382.9   85–18104
ISBN 0–88132–033–1

To Gardner Patterson—
Lifelong scholar and servant of the world trading system.

Preface

The merits of launching a major new round of international trade negotiations have been discussed extensively at least since 1982. The US administration, in particular, has attached high priority to the idea; President Ronald Reagan personally espoused it in major addresses, including his State of the Union message in January 1985. Such an initiative would continue the highly successful postwar pattern of conducting major negotiations in each decade: the Geneva Rounds in the 1940s and 1950s, the Dillon and Kennedy Rounds in the 1960s, and the Tokyo Round in the 1970s.

There has been surprisingly little analysis, however, of the possible substantive content of new trade talks; of possible themes for the effort, which could be used both to organize its conduct and to "sell" it politically around the world; and of negotiating strategies for moving it forward. The present study addresses all these questions, in an effort to enhance the precision of discussions of the issue and their relevance to all countries.

Several Institute studies, dating from *Trade Policy in the 1980s* (by myself and William R. Cline, November 1982), have recommended that new trade negotiations could be an important element in arresting the erosion of the open trading system. Other key elements, which are referred to in the present study but not discussed in depth, include a correction of the overvaluation of the dollar (described in several of our previous releases and analyzed comprehensively in *Deficits and the Dollar: The World Economy at Risk* by Stephen Marris, to be released shortly); a related improvement in the functioning of the international monetary regime (*The Exchange Rate System*, John Williamson, revised in June 1985); and better programs for domestic adjustment to trade dislocation (*Trade Policy for Troubled Industries*, Gary Clyde Hufbauer and Howard F. Rosen, to be released shortly). The present study offers a detailed appraisal of the needed trade negotiations themselves.

In carrying out their research, as with most projects at the Institute, the authors were assisted by a study group comprised of knowledgeable experts. The group included representatives of major American corporations, labor and agricultural interests, governmental agencies (including the Office of the US Trade Representative, Department of Commerce, Department of State, Treasury Department, Council of Economic Advisers, International Trade Commission, several congressional committees), and several major foreign countries. To help assure the needed international dimension, meetings on the study were also held in London, Paris, Brussels, Geneva, and Bellagio, with experts from both industrial and developing countries. The final draft of the study was rigorously reviewed by a number of outside experts, whose views were conveyed to the Director and taken into account in the final manuscript.

The Institute for International Economics is a private, nonprofit research institution for the study and discussion of international economic policy. Its purpose is to analyze important issues in that area and to develop and communicate practical new approaches for dealing with them.

The Institute was created in November 1981 through a generous commitment of funds from the German Marshall Fund of the United States. Support is being received from other private foundations and corporations, and the Institute is now broadening and diversifying its financial base. This particular study was partially funded by the John M. Olin Foundation, the McKnight Foundation, the Dayton Hudson Corporation, and Cargill, Inc.; their support is deeply appreciated.

The Board of Directors bears overall responsibility for the Institute and gives general guidance and approval to its research program—including identification of topics that are likely to become important to international economic policymakers over the medium run (generally, one to three years) and which thus should be addressed by the Institute. The Director of the Institute, working closely with the staff and outside Advisory Committee, is responsible for the development of particular projects and makes the final decision to publish an individual study. The Institute is completely nonpartisan.

The Institute hopes that its studies and other activities will contribute to building a stronger foundation for international economic policy around the world. Comments as to how it can best do so are invited from readers of these publications.

C. FRED BERGSTEN
Director
August 1985

viii

Contents

1   Introduction

In the early 1980s, just as the Tokyo Round agreements were taking force, the world economy was buffeted by a second oil shock, global recession, record levels of real interest rates, dramatic disinflation, and huge exchange rate movements. These events spawned a debt crisis in key developing countries and forced many to slash their imports. Record US trade deficits and a dollar that was badly overvalued prompted new protection for the American steel, textile, auto, sugar, and other industries. Despite huge trade surpluses and low unemployment, Japan barely accelerated the liberalization of its amply protected economy. Slow recovery in Europe left unemployment far above levels witnessed in the earlier postwar period, contributing to "Europessimism" and reinforcing European resistance to foreign competition.

In response to these woes, and despite pledges made at the Williamsburg (1983) and Versailles (1984) economic summits, the leading nations put their commitments to trade liberalization on the back burner. Instead, member countries of the Organization for Economic Cooperation and Development (OECD) increasingly managed trade to protect jobs, while developing countries rediscovered barter to supplement scarce foreign exchange.

Troubles in the Trading System

Indeed, the great international machinery devised in the 1940s seems to be breaking down. The Bretton Woods system of fixed exchange rates collapsed with the Smithsonian Agreement in 1971; the ensuing system of floating currencies has permitted much larger current account surpluses and deficits than those which brought down Bretton Woods. The International Monetary Fund (IMF) has ceded its central role in managing balance of payments deficits to the private banks, and the result is a more precarious system of international debt. After a burst of project lending in the McNamara years, the World Bank is running at a slower pace. And the General Agreement on

1

Tariffs and Trade (GATT), the framework of world trade rules, is noted more frequently for its shortcomings than its successes.

Against this dismal background, how ready is the world for the call issued at the 1985 Bonn Summit for a new round of trade talks?

The breadth and depth of economic problems may argue against moving too far too fast. Indeed, this was the French position at Bonn, and the French are not alone in expressing doubts. In an era when sharp changes in exchange rates, not trade reforms, seem to determine international competitiveness, key members of the US Congress have argued that negotiations should not advance until the dollar moves to more competitive levels. Many governments seem unprepared to reduce protection for important sectors such as steel, textiles and agriculture. Unemployment remains extremely high in Europe and Canada. The weakness of European high technology sectors prompts inward-looking policies. Less developed countries (LDCs)—many still facing massive debt burdens—seem reluctant to participate in new talks, much less to grant reciprocal trade concessions. Failed negotiations could badly harm an already weakened world trading system; indeed, the memory of the rancorous 1982 GATT Ministerial continues to cast doubt on the utility of far-reaching multilateral efforts.

There is thus very little enthusiasm for new trade talks. In the United States, firms that fear being "traded away" in negotiations far outnumber those that see something to gain. Much the same is true in other industrial countries. These attitudes are unlikely to change as long as the world economy staggers under high interest rates and low growth. In short, a much more buoyant macroeconomic climate is essential to stimulate enthusiasm for trade liberalization.

It can also be argued that the major trading nations need no new GATT round to attend to unfinished business. The LDCs, for example, ask that the United States and Europe simply respect their GATT obligations and eliminate trade barriers inconsistent with GATT, such as the Multi-Fiber Arrangement. The Europeans and Japanese point to US restraint agreements on steel as a GATT-illegal approach that the United States should address under its Versailles rollback commitment. The United States observes that the European common agricultural policy (CAP) represents a heavy drain on the European Community budget, entails dubious export subsidies, and denies US farmers their rightful export markets in Europe and third countries. Both the United States and Europe complain that Japanese liberalization is long overdue in telecommunications equipment and services, pharmaceuticals, semiconductors, wood and paper products, and various agricultural goods. The developed countries point to excessive reliance by the LDCs on quotas, exchange controls, and countertrade—practices that flaunt the spirit of GATT, even when they honor the letter of the agreements. All told, the agenda of unkept promises is very long.

While these are daunting obstacles, the dismal record of the 1980s, and the leftover problems of the 1970s, should be read neither as a litany of insurmountable obstacles nor as an agenda of recrimination, but rather as a call for energetic negotiations. The history of trade policy argues that momentum is vital: like a bicycle, the trading system either moves forward toward increased liberalization or it topples under protectionist pressures from sectoral interests. The pressures clearly are rising. The US Congress, for example, is now considering the imposition of a broad import surcharge and massive cutbacks in textile and apparel imports; scores of other protectionist bills also are in the hopper. The slow erosion of the trading rules witnessed since 1980 could easily accelerate unless meaningful forward progress is made.

Acting in isolation, few countries can muster sufficient internal political support to respect the full range of GATT disciplines. Acting in concert, many countries may be able to slow the drift toward protectionism, and even dismantle existing barriers.

New trade negotiations can do much to popularize the idea that trade promotes jobs and prosperity. This idea remains just as valid today as it was when David Ricardo wrote in 1817, or when the GATT system was devised in the 1940s. In the decades since World War II, trade has served as a locomotive for the world economy: trade has grown by 1 percentage point to 2.5 percentage points more per year than output (see Appendix). Indeed, in 1984, world production grew by about 5 percent, while trade grew by a robust 9 percent.[1] The expansion of trade stimulates growth by opening new markets for the exporting country and by freeing resources and stimulating productivity in the importing country. In short, liberal trade represents a supply-side policy for economic growth.

Appropriate demand-side policies are required to translate potential world growth into higher world output. Economic statesmen face a double challenge: first, to create the potential through trade liberalization; and second, to realize

---

1. GATT, "International Trade in 1984 and Current Prospects," GATT/1371, 14 March 1985.

that potential through wise macroeconomic policies.[2] In addition, major imbalances in the world economy must be addressed. The imperfect workings of the floating exchange rate system and the continuing threat of the LDC debt crisis cannot be ignored in the conduct of trade negotiations. A general synthesis of trade, money, and debt are needed for a better functioning world economy.

Parallel Negotiations

Recent events dramatically demonstrate the interrelationship between trade and money. The overvalued dollar, and resulting huge trade deficits, have fueled protectionist pressures in the United States. Uncertainties over exchange rates prompt many countries to question the relevance of trade talks. Meanwhile, the LDC debt crisis has drastically curtailed imports by developing countries. In 1981, the 16 most heavily indebted countries imported $202 billion; in 1984, this figure fell to $148 billion.[3]

Meaningful liberalization of the world trading system depends on better answers to the problems posed by exchange rates and LDC debt, even though these issues lie outside the range of traditional trade talks. Parallel negotiations seem to offer an appropriate format for handling such central questions.

FLOATING EXCHANGE RATES: MISALIGNMENT AND VOLATILITY

In the early 1970s, at the beginning of the postwar era of floating exchange rates, it was widely thought that a loss of trade competitiveness—resulting from a bout of inflation, outmoded products, or some other shock—would lead to exchange rate depreciation. In turn, a lower exchange rate would restore trade competitiveness.

As it turned out, in the period 1973–84, exchange rates behaved as

---

2. In the mid-1980s, appropriate policies would involve tax cuts in trade-surplus areas like Japan and Europe, and budget tightening and more expansive monetary policies in high-interest areas like the United States and Canada. See Stephen Marris, *Deficits and the Dollar: The World Economy at Risk,* POLICY ANALYSES IN INTERNATIONAL ECONOMICS (Washington: Institute for International Economics, forthcoming 1985).

3. GATT, "International Trade in 1984 and Current Prospects," p. 14.

expected only about half the time.[4] In retrospect this is not surprising, given the huge growth in international capital flows. Short-term capital flows, estimated at $40 trillion annually, have often swamped the effect of trade flows, amounting to $2 trillion annually.[5] Capital flows are influenced by many factors besides present or prospective trade deficits: confidence in the government, expectations about future exchange rates, interest rate differentials, profitable opportunities for direct investment, and stock market developments. The market play of these assorted forces contains no assurance that exchange rates will move, even in a rough fashion over the medium term, to ensure current account equilibrium.

Thus, in the first quarter of 1985, the trade-weighted dollar exchange rate was some 35 percent overvalued compared with a level that would lead to an approximately balanced US current account position. Likewise, the mark and the yen were both about 10 percent undervalued on a trade-weighted basis.[6] If currency relations stayed at these levels, the US current account deficit could reach $300 billion by 1990.[7]

Secondary to the problem of fundamental misalignment is the problem of wide fluctuations over short periods of time. For example, between November 9, 1984 and February 23, 1985, the mark dropped by about 17 percent against the dollar. From February 23, 1985 to April 19, 1985, however, the situation reversed and the mark strengthened against the dollar by about 15 percent. Such volatility has increased over the past decade, not only because of the advent of floating exchange rates, but also because of liberalized capital markets and advances in information technologies and telecommuni-

---

4. Gary Clyde Hufbauer, "Floating Exchange Rates, Trade Deficits, and Budget Deficits." (Statement before US Senate Committee on Finance, Hearings on the Role of Floating Exchange Rates in the International Trading System, 23 April 1985).

5. *Wall Street Journal*, 30 July 1985, p. 1. Short-term capital flows largely involve a trade in the morning that is reversed in the afternoon. The data on gross short-term capital flows are notoriously rough.

6. For the basic approach to calculating equilibrium exchange rates, see John Williamson, *The Exchange Rate System*, POLICY ANALYSES IN INTERNATIONAL ECONOMICS 5 rev. ed. (Washington: Institute for International Economics, June 1985). In the first quarter of 1985, the bilateral yen/dollar rate was about 20 percent undervalued, while the bilateral mark/dollar rate was about 30 percent undervalued.

7. Marris, *Deficits and the Dollar*.

cations.[8] The combination of misalignment and volatility significantly increases the cost of foreign trade and makes planning more difficult.

France has insisted on parallel monetary talks to address the problems of misalignment and volatility.[9] This initiative recalls a similar theme that France promoted at the launching of the Tokyo Round. In 1985, however, France and the rest of Europe can claim strong allies within the US business community and in the US Congress. Prestigious groups such as the Business Roundtable and the National Association of Manufacturers have called for steps to deal with the "super dollar," ranging from reduction of the US budget deficit to greater cooperation among the central banks of the key currency countries.[10] Influential senators, such as John C. Danforth (R-Missouri)[11] and Lloyd M. Bentsen (D-Texas),[12] have put monetary reform at the top of the international agenda. The experience of the past five years has created enormous disillusion about the workings of a floating exchange rate system. Until these concerns are addressed, the process of reducing trade barriers will be stalled.

---

8. Williamson, *The Exchange Rate System*, pp. 12–13.

9. *New York Times*, 28 March 1985, p. A1. In April 1985, Treasury Secretary James A. Baker III proposed a new high-level world monetary conference to be held in late 1985 or early 1986, but later said that there would be no departure from the substance of the previous US commitment to market-determined exchange rates. By the time of the Bonn summit in May 1985, France gave greater priority to preserving the European Community agricultural system than to reforming the world monetary system. The possibility of a world monetary conference was thus left as a dangling proposition. Finance ministers of the major industrial nations recommended more modest procedural reforms in June 1985.

10. Alexander B. Trowbridge, National Association of Manufacturers, "America's Role in the Global Economy," *Hearings before the Senate Committee on Foreign Relations*, 99 Cong., 1 sess., 6 March 1985, p. 11. The Business Roundtable has sounded similar themes in its statement on a new trade round, included in "Chairmen's Report on a New Round of Multilateral Trade Negotiations," *Advisory Committee for Trade Negotiations*, submitted to the United States Trade Representative, 15 May 1985.

11. Senator John C. Danforth, "United States Trade Policy" (Address to the National Press Club, Washington, 25 April 1985).

12. Senate Democratic Working Group on Trade Policy, Senator Lloyd M. Bentsen, Chairman, *The New Global Economy: First Steps in a United States Trade Strategy* (Washington, April 1985; preliminary report).

The precise outcome of monetary negotiations cannot be foreseen. In broad terms, however, the goal is to limit the risk of severe misalignment of exchange rates between the four major currencies—the dollar, the mark,[13] the yen, and the pound sterling—and to moderate the extent of volatility.

"Misalignment" may be defined as a disparity between the actual exchange rate and a rate that would produce current account equilibrium, taking into account a sustainable level of net inflows or outflows of capital.[14] In the first instance, official steps might be taken to correct a major currency only when two conditions are fulfilled: the currency is misaligned to the extent of 10 percent or more; and the misalignment operates to push the country's current account position away from its long-term equilibrium rather than toward its long-term equilibrium. For example, if the dollar was 20 percent overvalued and the US current account showed a substantial deficit, official steps would be taken to reduce the exchange value of the dollar. On the other hand, if the dollar was 20 percent undervalued and the US current account showed a substantial deficit, no steps would be taken, since the undervaluation would be pushing the current account position toward equilibrium.[15]

"Volatility" refers to abrupt short-term movements in exchange rates. Central banks might curb volatility by issuing more explicit guidelines as to when they see cause for concern in "disorderly" foreign exchange markets. For example, once exchange rates again approach their long-term equilibrium levels, movements in excess of 5 percent within a week might be defined as "disorderly," and thus likely to attract official intervention. Knowledge of these guidelines would do much to restrain bandwagon speculation.

When circumstances indicate the need for official action, the armory of measures could include at least three weapons. In the first instance, central banks might voice public displeasure with prevailing exchange rates and shift their reserves away from the overvalued currency and into undervalued currencies. Ordinarily, this measure alone should cope with volatility and

---

13. Depending on developments in the European monetary system, the focus might be on the European Currency Unit (ECU) instead of on just the mark.

14. Williamson, *The Exchange Rate System.*

15. Such a policy would entail a modest first step in the direction of target zones for exchange rate intervention advocated by John Williamson. If a situation arose in which the dollar was undervalued by 20 percent, while the US current account was in *persistent* deficit, the reference calculation of the equilibrium exchange rate might well be adjusted.

help correct misalignment. Next, countries with overvalued currencies might increase their money supplies more rapidly while countries with undervalued currencies might decrease the rate of growth of their money supplies. This adjustment in the *composition* of world money supply, while keeping the stock of world money approximately constant, could moderate exchange rates without triggering inflation or deflation.[16] Finally, and politically most difficult, countries could agree to consult with a view to adjusting the size of national fiscal surpluses and deficits to counter pressure in the exchange markets.

DEVELOPING-COUNTRY DEBT

Through the end of 1981, the developing countries taken as a group enjoyed a huge net inflow of funds from international banks. New loans and new credit lines far exceeded interest and principal payments. As a result, by the end of 1981, LDC external debt reached $550 billion. The debt crisis broke in 1982 when LDC export earnings plummeted and real interest rates vaulted to record levels. Soon "involuntary lending" became the rule: international banks reluctantly rolled over principal and funded interest. In fact, since 1982, the international banks would have demanded far larger repayments if they could have done so without pushing their LDC clients into default.

As long as the OECD economy expands an average 3 percent annually in real terms, and as long as interest rates do not flare up, many of the indebted LDCs should be able to "grow out" of their debts, with occasional rescheduling along the way. This means that, in severe cases, debt-export ratios will decline from a range of 250 percent to 400 percent to 200 percent and below. As the nominal volume of debt declines relative to exports, the financial community will come to feel more comfortable about its LDC exposure and involuntary lending will shade into voluntary lending.[17]

Even in this optimistic scenario, however, indebted countries are asked to divert most of the gain in export earnings to the service of debt. This diversion

---

16. Ronald I. McKinnon, *An International Standard for Monetary Stabilization,* POLICY ANALYSES IN INTERNATIONAL ECONOMICS 8 (Washington: Institute for International Economics, March 1984).

17. William R. Cline, *International Debt: Systemic Risk and Policy Response* (Washington: Institute for International Economics, especially ch. 8).

implies little increase in imports and furnishes a source of continuing pressure on the trading system. Many LDCs have little latitude, and even less inclination, to relax a whole series of measures taken to restrain imports, including highly restrictive quotas, extraordinarily high tariffs, barter arrangements, and buy-national procurement programs. These attitudes are unfortunate, because more relaxed import policies could soon result in higher growth. According to one set of estimates, a 10 percent growth in imports would, on average, increase Latin American GDP by 2.5 percent to 5.0 percent.[18] In the short run, however, more imports mean a weaker current account position and still greater debt. What is needed is additional finance, both as an incentive for liberal policies and as a bridge to larger LDC export sales.

The most practical source for additional finance is new credit from the international financial institutions plus debt-service relief through longer debt rescheduling terms.[19] These measures should be linked to trade liberalization. Traditionally, the IMF, the World Bank, and the regional development banks (together, the international financial institutions, or IFIs) have carried on their business largely independent of GATT concerns. Moreover, debt rescheduling talks have usually concentrated on financial flows, almost to the exclusion of trade policy concerns. The close connection between highly restrictive LDC trade policies and external debt burdens suggests that closer links should now be forged between trade talks, IFI lending, and debt rescheduling.

In practice, how would the linkage work? At one extreme, the linkage might depend entirely on the enlightened good intentions of the LDCs. The developed countries would grant additional resources to the IMF and to the World Bank, and the private banks would agree to multiyear reschedulings— all in hopes that the availability of additional finance would prompt developing

---

18. C. Fred Bergsten, William R. Cline, and John Williamson, *Bank Lending to Developing Countries: The Policy Alternatives*, POLICY ANALYSES IN INTERNATIONAL ECONOMICS 10 (Washington: Institute for International Economics, 1985), p. 209 and the annex.

19. Bergsten, Cline, and Williamson, *Bank Lending to Developing Countries*. It is also conceivable that national export credit agencies might agree on a coordinated expansion of direct credits and loan guarantees to indebted developing countries. Traditionally, however, official export credit agencies, such as the US Export–Import Bank and the French COFACE, have acted as bitter rivals, not as joint venturers.

countries to adopt more liberal trade policies. At the other extreme, all new IMF and World Bank loans and all further rescheduling agreements would contain stringent trade liberalization preconditions.

Each of these extremes raises its own objections. One looks like a wishful carrot; the other, a heavy stick. Between these two extremes, a middle ground might find some portion of IFI funds and some part of rescheduling agreements tied to trade liberalization commitments.

As an illustration of the middle road, the industrial countries could assemble a five-year package of $5 billion to $10 billion a year of new money financed through a general capital increase for the World Bank.[20] The funds would be disbursed under structural adjustment loans, with liberalizing strings attached, to countries in balance of payments difficulty.[21] Such an approach has already achieved important trade liberalization in countries like Korea. In recent years, Korea has received $550 million contingent on both sharp reductions in tariff rates (these reductions would bring the average tariff from about 24 percent in 1983 to 18 percent in 1988) and a substantial increase in the number of goods subject to automatic import approval. The World Bank has promoted similar reforms in countries like the Philippines, Turkey, Morocco, Ivory Coast, and Jamaica. All told, the resources committed to these countries are about $1 billion per year; thus, there is room for a considerable enlargement of the approach.

Alternatively, the IMF could go forward with a major allocation of special drawing rights (SDRs). In turn, the industrial countries would lend a major portion of their own allocations back to the IMF for on-lending to those developing countries that agreed to liberalize trade policies significantly.[22]

---

20. For a detailed analysis of World Bank capital requirements which also suggests an expansion of this magnitude, see Donald R. Lessard and John Williamson, *Financial Intermediation Beyond the Debt Crisis*, POLICY ANALYSES IN INTERNATIONAL ECONOMICS (Washington: Institute for International Economics, forthcoming 1985).

21. In April 1985, for example, the US Treasury agreed that the World Bank could exceed the previously established 10 percent limit on its funds available for balance of payments purposes.

22. This idea was proposed by the Overseas Development Council, "Small Debtors, Big Problems: the Quiet Crisis," *Policy Focus*, 1985, no. 2, p. 5. The major industrial countries have not been receptive, however, to recent proposals for a new SDR allocation; instead they have called for "a comprehensive review of the future role of the SDR in the system." See *Communiqué of the Ministers and Governors of the Group of Ten*, Tokyo, 21 June 1985.

Likewise, in the context of rescheduling agreements, private banks could add an extra two or three years to the maturity term, conditioned on specified trade reforms.

An illustration of the liberalization approach that might be followed is provided by Mexico's 1985 letter of intent to the IMF on the third year of its austerity program. According to the letter of intent, the cumbersome Mexican system of import licenses would be gradually replaced by tariffs. Meanwhile, exporters would be allowed to import up to 40 percent of the value of their exports free of import licenses, tariffs, and value-added taxes.[23]

In order to complete the link to trade talks, developing countries that implemented liberalization programs should be able to claim negotiating "credit" for increases in imports over a base period level that are reasonably attributable to the liberalization. For example, if Peru undertook an import liberalization program in 1985 and Peru's imports of liberalized goods rose from $1.0 billion to $1.5 billion in 1987, Peru could claim credit for concessions worth $500 million in the context of multilateral trade talks. If Peru did not receive comparable concessions, it could impose "snapback" restrictions on its imports. The GATT Secretariat should play a role in drawing up the liberalization plans and afterwards in monitoring the results and certifying the value of developing-country concessions for future trade talks.

A system of liberal trade can best realize its supply-side potential in a world of buoyant growth and balanced demand. In the mid-1980s, growth is weak and current accounts are badly imbalanced. These circumstances highlight the interrelationships between trade, money, and debt, and the need to supplement the mechanisms of the IMF, the World Bank, and the GATT. In the chapters that follow, we assume that growth is stimulated, and that imbalances in money and debt are addressed in parallel negotiations.[24] Those assumptions, in reality preconditions for successful trade talks, enable us to focus on the trade policy story.

---

23. *Journal of Commerce*, 27 March 1985, p. 7B. The program has been subsequently revised; exporters now are allowed to import only 30 percent of the value of their exports free of import licenses.

24. "Parallel" does not necessarily imply step-by-step progress. Decisions and implementing measures would likely be taken on different timetables.

2   Strategies and Players

Trade talks need a bold "theme" to realize their full potential. The theme should generate political interest in launching new talks and inspire meaningful bargains as negotiations progress.

Prior trade rounds had explicit unifying themes: for example, the Kennedy Round represented a frontal attack on tariffs; the Tokyo Round went one step farther and sought new discipline on nontariff barriers. The next round has several tasks: it must achieve a standstill on existing trade restrictions; it must confront sophisticated means of government intervention and protection, for example, through countertrade and procurement; it must work to liberalize trade in difficult sectors such as agriculture, steel, and textiles; it must develop new rules to govern trade in services and high technology products; and, above all, it should highlight the mutual benefit of open trade to all member countries of the General Agreement on Tariffs and Trade (GATT).

A growth theme captures these diverse tasks. The purpose of lowering trade barriers and "leveling the playing field" is to make national economies more efficient, thereby adding to their capacity for growth. A "Growth Round" suggests the extension of the national treatment principle to foreign suppliers in diverse areas ranging from insurance to pharmaceutical testing. A Growth Round encompasses the full integration of key developing countries into the trading system, on differing schedules depending on their circumstances. And a Growth Round points to the phased reduction and eventual elimination by developed countries of all border measures, leading to the inauguration of talks on an industrial free trade area by the year 2000. In thinking about a round, however, it is important to realize that it will not conclude all at once; instead there are likely to be numerous way stations on the liberalization path.

Seven Strategic Goals

To realize its theme, the Growth Round needs to build on seven strategic goals, many left over from the Tokyo Round. *First,* countries should agree

12

to a meaningful standstill with implementing "teeth" on new barriers to merchandise trade. *Second*, the principles of the GATT system should be extended to cover key new areas such as services, investment, and intellectual property. *Third*, quantitative restrictions (QRs) should be replaced, whenever possible, by tariffs or auctioned quotas, and the revenues should be dedicated to adjustment. *Fourth*, the growth in demand for the products of troubled industries such as sugar, dairy, apparel, and steel, should be satisfied by the most competitive producer in the world economy. *Fifth*, the principles of fair trade should be enlarged to cover new areas of abuse such as subsidies that "steal" third-country markets and commercial counterfeiting. *Sixth*, in order to promote meaningful participation by all GATT members, concessions outside the tariff area should be accorded on a conditional most-favored-nation (MFN) basis. *Seventh*, concessions should be implemented on schedules that take account of national current account surpluses and deficits.

STANDSTILL WITH TEETH

The experience of the 1980s has shown that each country is tempted to restrict trade for reasons of overriding national importance. In the United States, an overvalued dollar and soaring imports are viewed as imperatives calling for trade protection both for particular industries, such as steel and textiles, and more broadly for the entire traded goods sector. Developing countries, such as Brazil, believe that protection of infant computer industries and other high technology products are vital ingredients of industrial and national security policy. Europe seeks to create a common telecommunications market for its own suppliers before letting foreign producers join the party. Japan wants both to insulate its declining industries—such as steel, textiles, and petroleum refining—from import competition, and to catch up with US technology in aircraft, software, and pharmaceuticals production.

The proper answer to these tendencies is a mutual commitment by key GATT members to a standstill on new merchandise trade restrictions. Such an agreement should be implemented at the start of a new round of negotiations and should be applied to the trade of all participating countries. A major purpose of the new standstill agreement would be to discourage ingenious new import barriers that violate the spirit, and barely observe the letter, of the GATT. Some of these restrictions are designed for protective purposes, such as tailored standards for telecommunications equipment; others are inspired by an urge to create bargaining chips for a new negotiation; and still others, such as countertrade requirements, are necessitated by foreign exchange constraints.

Unlike past attempted standstills—ranging from Organization for Economic Cooperation and Development (OECD) trade pledges to summit declarations— which often were violated soon after they were negotiated, a new standstill would have to be closely monitored and enforced. Any country should be able to notify violations that infringe on its trading interests to a "Standstill Panel" operating under GATT auspices. In addition, the GATT Secretariat should be empowered to notify the panel of any violations not otherwise brought to its attention.

Only two exceptions should be permitted to the standstill on merchandise trade. First, escape clause actions taken in full observance of GATT Article XIX safeguard rules should be permitted and should *not* be subject to retaliation or compensation requirements. This exception would encourage a rediscovery of Article XIX as the principle vehicle for relief from import competition. Conformity with Article XIX standards—appropriate degree and causation of injury, trade relief consistent with the MFN principle, relief degressive over time—would be verified by ex post review by the Standstill Panel.

Second, normal countervailing duty, antidumping duty, and similar unfair trade countermeasures also should be permitted, as long as they are taken in accordance with the GATT and the relevant GATT codes. As to other new trade restrictions falling outside these exceptions, the Standstill Panel could provide a fast-track enforcement mechanism, recommending compensation or authorizing retaliation.[1]

The standstill commitment should also apply to all countertrade require- ments on import transactions valued over, say, $10 million. Countries facing balance of payments problems should not be bound by this prohibition; nonetheless, they should notify these transactions to the Standstill Panel.[2]

---

1. A similar proposal for a standstill was put forward in the context of the 1982 GATT Ministerial. See C. Fred Bergsten and William R. Cline, *Trade Policy in the 1980s*, POLICY ANALYSES IN INTERNATIONAL ECONOMICS 3 (Washington: Institute for International Economics, 1982), pp. 66–70.

2. Transparency would be an important first step in controlling the spread of countertrade requirements. See Michael R. Czinkota and Anne Talbot, "GATT Regulation of Countertrade: Issues and Prospects," National Center for Export-Import Studies, Staff Paper No. 20 (Washington, July 1985).

The standstill on merchandise trade would not automatically extend to services, for the simple reason that the GATT framework does not now extend to services. Instead, a services standstill should be developed during the negotiations in the larger context of a new framework of rules.

BROADER COVERAGE OF GATT PRINCIPLES

GATT rules do not now apply to a large segment of trade. Textiles and apparel and agriculture are technically, but not effectively, under GATT coverage. Except in minor ways, services and trade-related investment issues are excluded, as are commercial counterfeiting (an issue raised during the Tokyo Round) and other intellectual property questions. Much high technology trade is exempted from GATT discipline because of national security safeguards or government procurement exclusions. Indeed, by some accounts, less than half of international trade is conducted according to the principles of GATT.[3]

The expansion of the trade coverage of GATT rules should be a major strategic goal of the Growth Round. In some areas, such as government procurement of surface transportation or telecommunications equipment and acceptance of foreign pharmaceuticals test data, immediate progress can be made by extension of the appropriate GATT codes. In other areas, such as agriculture and textiles, long transition periods will be necessary before the normal disciplines can apply. In still other areas, such as traded services and commercial counterfeiting, new means to discipline international transactions need to be devised in the GATT framework. Whatever the specifics, the strategic goal is to bring a much larger portion of world trade under the GATT umbrella.

RETARIFFICATION PLUS ADJUSTMENT

A new round of international trade talks is not going to succeed unless it can make progress toward liberalization in difficult sectors such as textiles and

---

3. A recent study suggested that only 5 percent of world trade respects GATT rules, a figure that seems unbelievably low. See Senate Democratic Working Group on Trade Policy, Senator Lloyd M. Bentsen, Chairman, *The New Global Economy: First Steps in a United States Trade Strategy* (Washington, April 1985; preliminary report), p. 13.

apparel, steel, dairy, and pharmaceuticals. After all, these are the areas where huge trade growth is possible, both among the developed countries and between developed and developing countries, and where potential efficiency gains from expanded trade are most conspicuous. And, not surprisingly, these are the areas where trade abrasion has been greatest.

To move forward, negotiations must reconcile the political strength and legitimate demands of troubled industries with the call for economic efficiency and trade liberalization. To date, instead of adjusting to persistent changes in comparative advantage, national policy officials often opt for semipermanent QRs that selectively limit imports from a few aggressive suppliers. Along the way, the safeguard principles of GATT Article XIX are forgotten. Those principles call for temporary[4] (not permanent) "breathing room" protection through the use of tariffs or quotas that are applied in an even-handed fashion (respecting the MFN principle) against all foreign suppliers (not selectively against a few countries). Because adequate adjustment alternatives have not been put forward, governments have constructed instead a web of quantitative restraints designed both to limit imports and to keep domestic prices well above their international levels.

Experience has shown that jobs are not permanently saved, nor farm adjustment indefinitely avoided, when trade barriers are imposed. With or without trade protection, jobs in troubled industries are lost, and farms are mechanized and consolidated.[5] But protection does influence the rate of change. Thus, it is not a question whether industries and workers will eventually adjust, but how great will be the pain and how fast the process. Appropriate government transition assistance can work as an alternative to protection in easing the pain and speeding the process.

"Retariffication plus adjustment" is clumsy shorthand for an elegant idea: replace QRs with tariffs or auctioned quotas and dedicate the revenue to domestic adjustment. What this means is that quota rents, resulting from government-inspired scarcity, would be collected by the importing country's treasury and used to promote adjustment. In practical terms this would mean

---

4. GATT Article XIX:1 (a) reads ". . . for such time as may be necessary to prevent or remedy such injury. . . ."

5. Gary Clyde Hufbauer and Howard F. Rosen, *Trade Policy for Troubled Industries*, POLICY ANALYSES IN INTERNATIONAL ECONOMICS (Washington: Institute for International Economics, forthcoming 1985), ch. 2, 5.

liberal retraining (coupled with income maintenance) and early retirement programs for workers who choose to leave, and financial assistance for firms that choose to downsize by paring inefficient capacity. As earmarked funds are used by the industry to adapt to changing market conditions, more quotas can be sold at auction or the tariff can be lowered.

In industries that have a long history of protection, reciprocal international concessions will be critical for this linked approach to trade liberalization and adjustment. National adjustment programs are unlikely to be undertaken in the absence of comparable commitments in competing countries. Indeed, no country should be asked to bear a disproportionate adjustment burden in stagnant industries if other countries with similar problems do not follow suit.

Retariffication would end the distortion and discrimination that arise whenever markets are parcelled out by government fiat rather than through the workings of the price system. Dedication of the revenue for adjustment would ensure that resources are available to make the transition to freer trade. The combination of retariffication and adjustment represents a central strategy for pursuing trade liberalization in difficult areas such as dairy, steel, and apparel.

MARKET PRINCIPLES AT THE MARGIN

As a companion and supplement to the "retariffication plus adjustment" strategy, the *growth* in demand for the products of troubled industries now protected by import restraints should be served according to market principles. At the margin, the price mechanism rather than fiat would be used to allocate scarce import rights. The combined strategy of retariffication, adjustment, and market principles at the margin would help revive original GATT safeguard principles.

This approach could be implemented in a variety of ways. For example, governments could agree to stop subsidizing larger and larger levels of output under domestic farm programs. Instead, they would agree to cap assistance at a fixed level of production and force producers to market any additional output at market prices. As another example, West German steel producers have proposed (unsuccessfully to date) the gradual reduction of minimum price levels and the combination of quotas for groups of steel items.[6] These

6. *Financial Times,* 22 March 1985, p. 18.

proposals illustrate ways that market principles might gradually supplant bureaucratic directives in heavily regulated industries.

EXTENDING THE RULES OF FAIR TRADE

Any firm that loses market share or faces price pressure from imports is tempted to cry unfair competition. Often complaints should be channeled into adjustment efforts, but sometimes they are genuine and require redress. Unfair practices that go uncorrected can threaten "innocent" as well as "guilty" trade. For example, the recent movement toward cartelization of world steel trade stems from a reluctance by the United States and the European Community (EC) in the 1970s to impose countervailing duties against subsidized imports and to downsize their industries to the viable core. Instead, both subsidized and unsubsidized trade is now subject to QRs in the United States and in Europe.

Four fairness issues now head the agenda: widespread subsidies, misuse of intellectual property, extravagantly unbalanced concessions, and human rights in the workplace.

The fairness issue behind the subsidies debate is quite simple: most private business owners regard it as unfair to be thrown into competition with a foreign treasury. In the Tokyo Round, progress was made on limiting export subsidies, but enormous loopholes still remain for creative government intervention. The task in the Growth Round is to strengthen the fabric against the use of subsidies while not erecting an armada of contingent protection that can be easily deployed to impede the flow of trade.

The fairness issue involved in the misuse of intellectual property is this: it seems wrong for an opportunistic competitor to "pirate" technology or designs that were patented or copyrighted in the country of invention, and to use that knowledge to produce goods for sale in the pirate's home country or a third-country market.

The fairness question behind unbalanced concessions can be illustrated by three examples. It seems inherently unfair for public telecommunications monopolies to buy only from domestic suppliers when private telecommunications firms in other countries purchase components from abroad. Similarly, countries with an efficient agricultural sector, such as Australia, Argentina, and Canada, find the lax rules on export subsidies for agricultural goods unbalanced when compared to the prohibition on export subsidies for industrial products. Likewise, British shoe manufacturers are outraged at a 175 percent tariff on exports to Brazil, when they must compete against Brazilian shoes sold in the British market that pay a tariff of only 15 percent.[7]

The fairness issue with labor involves basic human rights: forced labor, right to organize, minimum working age, and acceptable working conditions (including minimum wages, working hours, and health and safety provisions). Many of these issues have been addressed by various International Labor Organization (ILO) conventions.[8] More recently, the US Trade and Tariff Act of 1984 mandated consideration of human rights conditions in the determination of eligibility under the US generalized system of preferences.

Participants on both sides of the fairness debate are quick to recognize that the concept of unfair trade is dangerously elastic.[9] Fairness is in the eyes of the beholder; no matter how much progress is made, some participants will always find unfairness in the world trading system. Pushed to absurd lengths, the fairness strategy could point to a modern version of the "scientific tariff," namely, a tariff designed to equalize all differences in the cost of production and thus remove much of the basis of trade. Protagonists of fair trade have not yet carried their argument to such extremes. They merely insist that egregious practices be subject to better international discipline. This seems reasonable. As long as unfair practices are defined in a multilateral context, rather than on a unilateral basis, the dangers of runaway unfair trade protection can be avoided.

THE CONDITIONAL MFN PRINCIPLE

The most-favored-nation principle is often regarded as the cornerstone of the GATT system.[10] It averts the bad political feelings that might erupt if country

---

7. This example was cited by a business group in London. Comparable stories of unbalanced tariffs are told about many developing countries, such as India and Mexico, and about a few developed countries, such as Australia.

8. Steve Charnovitz, "The Human Rights of Foreign Labor," *Worldview*, January 1985.

9. Practices sometimes identified as unfair include: more relaxed antitrust constraints or environmental controls than those imposed in the United States or in Europe; health insurance packages paid through public funding, rather than through private payrolls; and very different wage rates in South Korea or India as compared to Japan, Canada, or the United States.

10. GATT, *International Trade 1983/84*, pp. 20–22.

A offered greater concessions to country B than to country C. It encourages exports from the most competitive suppliers and thus maximizes economic efficiency. It facilitates tariff liberalization by preserving the balance of negotiated concessions.[11] In general, the MFN principle safeguards the interests of third countries whose trade prospects might otherwise be damaged by bilateral and plurilateral trade pacts.

The issue in the Growth Round is not the broad merits of an MFN approach. The issue is whether new rules and obligations should be extended on an *unconditional* basis to all existing GATT members, or whether they should be granted on a *conditional* basis only to those countries that make concessions in return.

The first six GATT rounds were mainly concerned with tariff cutting, and tariff concessions were extended on an unconditional MFN basis to all GATT members. This approach worked well as long as the great bulk of world trade was conducted among the United States, Canada, Western Europe, and Japan, and as long as each of the major players made substantial concessions to the bargain.

Difficulties arose when the impact of the "free rider" and the "foot dragger" became more acute. The classic free rider is a small country that makes no concessions itself, enjoys the benefits of concessions made by others, but is not a major exporter. In isolation, no single free rider engenders much of a burden, but troubles arise if a number of individually small free riders become collectively large enough to create a significant leakage when benefits are extended on an unconditional MFN basis. The foot dragger is a country which is so large that no agreement can be reached if it does not join a multilateral negotiation. For example, it would be difficult for the United States and Japan to talk about unconditional MFN access to telephone procurement without the presence of Europe.

In an unconditional MFN system, free riders and foot draggers can severely inhibit the granting of concessions, thus buttressing existing trade barriers. It is no exaggeration to say that free riders and foot draggers are debilitating the whole GATT system. In the Tokyo Round, the problems of free riders and foot draggers caused the United States to depart from the unconditional MFN approach in some important codes, notably those relating to subsidies

---

11. A concession loses part of its value if the granting country can later offer a better deal to a third country.

and government procurement, and to insist that code benefits be available only to code signatories, not to free riders.

The conditional MFN approach was not as great a heresy as it might seem, however. The GATT itself is a conditional MFN agreement whose provisions apply only among signatories. There were only 23 founding countries (excluding, for example, Germany, Italy, and Japan). Even today, the GATT excludes important trading nations such as Mexico, Venezuela, Saudi Arabia, China, and the Soviet Union.

Much wider use of the conditional MFN approach will be required if bargains are to be struck in the Growth Round, issue by issue and year by year. It is hard to imagine a liberalization of steel or textile trade that would accord unconditional MFN entry into the American, Japanese, and European markets by India, Brazil, and Korea unless those countries made very significant concessions of their own. Dairy and sugar trade, both tightly regulated by QRs, can only be liberalized if all countries that stand to gain larger markets are prepared to make significant concessions. A conditional MFN approach would enable, for example, a US-Canadian-Japanese bargain on telecommunications to be struck, say, in 1988, and permit the Europeans to hold off joining until, say 1992, when they received reciprocal concessions in agreements on carbon steel and dairy.[12] Similar opportunities for a conditional MFN approach exist in North-South trade.[13]

The strongest argument against the conditional MFN approach is that it might lead to fragmentation of the world trading system and to regionalization of political alliances. These dangers can be minimized if two important limits are respected in the use of a conditional MFN approach to deal with free riders and foot draggers. First, tariffs should not be applied on a conditional MFN basis among GATT members. The GATT Article I principle of unconditional MFN tariff rates is a foundation stone that should not be disturbed. Second, all conditional MFN codes should be open to all countries.

---

12. Chapter 4 advocates "continuing negotiations" with a rolling agenda, where each step is conditioned on subsequent progress in later talks.

13. An individual developing country is seldom the principal supplier of EC, US, or Japanese imports that are limited by quantitative restraints. Thus, individual developing countries might have little interest in paying for MFN liberalization, but they might be very much interested in conditional MFN bargains. See, for example, L. Alan Winters, "Negotiating the Removal of Non-Tariff Barriers," Discussion Paper Report DRD115, Development Research Department (World Bank, Washington, March 1985; processed).

Conditional MFN should not be used as a means of forming exclusive "inner clubs"; instead, the terms of admission should be no higher for new members than for founding members.

CONCESSIONS LINKED TO CURRENT ACCOUNTS

Traditionally, each country in a trade bargain has agreed to implement trade concessions at approximately the same pace.[14] This rule works well as long as current account imbalances are transitory, corrected within a short period by exchange rate movements. But that has not been the case in the 1980s. In a world with huge and persistent current account imbalances, it is unrealistic to expect trade concessions to be implemented on a parallel schedule by both deficit and surplus countries.

Experience in Europe with the Code of Liberalisation in the 1940s and 1950s offers a lesson for the problems of the 1980s and 1990s. Beset by payments difficulties after World War II, many European countries resorted to quantitative restrictions to manage their trade. New mechanisms had to be invented to enable Europe to emerge from these self-defeating restraints. The Code of Liberalisation required member countries of the Organization for European Economic Cooperation (OEEC) to liberalize, by October 1950, a minimum of 60 percent of private imports in each of three sectors (food and feedstuffs, raw materials, and manufactured products). By February 1951, 75 percent of total private imports were to be liberalized. Countries with payments difficulties were, however, allowed to defer their liberalizing measures without retaliation by other European nations. In January 1955, the requisite degree of liberalization was increased from 75 percent to 90 percent for all private imports, and from a minimum of 60 percent to 75 percent for each of the three sectors. Again, an escape clause was provided both for balance of payments difficulties and for reasons of "national importance or equity."[15]

This experience demonstrates that stronger countries can contribute to trade

---

14. There have always been limited exceptions to the traditional rule for LDCs and for difficult sectors such as textiles.

15. Organization for European Economic Cooperation, *A Decade of Co-operation: Achievements and Perspectives* (Paris, April 1958).

liberalization in an accelerated fashion. This lesson should be made a regular part of the Growth Round. Countries with current account surpluses should be called upon to implement their concessions ahead of deficit countries, and this obligation should be recognized in an appropriate formula. Under pressure from the United States and the European Community, Japan already has accelerated implementation of its Tokyo Round tariff cuts in an effort to spur imports.[16] The proposed US Trade Emergency and Export Promotion Act of 1985, sponsored by a group of Democratic congressmen, also seeks liberalization commitments from trade-surplus countries, though the architecture of its approach is flawed.[17]

The Players

The Growth Round will involve scores of countries and dozens of issues. But negotiations can be successfully launched once consensus is reached among a few key players. With this in mind, the following section examines the negotiating concerns of the United States, the European Community, Japan, the key less developed countries (LDCs), and the smaller industrial countries (Canada, the Nordics, Switzerland, and Australia).

THE UNITED STATES

For the next several years the US approach to trade negotiations will be colored by the macroeconomic environment.[18] The US current account deficit exceeded $100 billion in 1984. If the dollar remains at its fourth quarter

---

16. On 25 June 1985, Japan announced a 20 percent tariff cut on about 1,800 products, a small step toward reducing the huge Japanese current account surplus. See *Washington Post,* 26 June 1985, p. D1.

17. *Washington Post,* 18 July 1985, p. A1. The proposed act defines trade-surplus countries by excluding petroleum trade, ignoring LDC debt-servicing obligations, and emphasizing bilateral trade balances with the United States.

18. See, for example, C. Fred Bergsten, "The Second Debt Crisis Is Coming," *Challenge,* vol. 28, no. 2 (May/June 1985), pp. 14–21; and the statements by Senators Lloyd M. Bentsen and John C. Danforth noted in chapter 1.

1984 level, even if US economic growth slows below the rest of the OECD for the remainder of the 1980s, American current account deficits could reach $300 billion by 1990, about 5 percent of projected GNP at that time.[19] Based on this projection, the net external financial debt of the United States would reach $1.3 trillion by 1990. In 1988, the US external debt-export ratio would exceed 200 percent, a point that has often triggered debt crises in other countries. Even if a major dollar correction were to begin promptly, the US trade figures would show little improvement before 1987.

Meanwhile, the dollar overvaluation effectively taxes all American exports by about 35 percent and subsidizes all imports coming into the country by a like amount. Not only are export markets sacrificed and sales lost to imports; but equally important, prices realized by the traded goods sector in the domestic market are badly depressed. On the assumption that 25 percent of US output competes with international goods, and that a 35 percent dollar overvaluation translates on average into price suppression of only 10 percent, the adverse effect on business earnings in the production of traded goods has perhaps reached $100 billion.[20]

The punishing effect that the overvalued dollar exerts on the traded-goods sector will eventually be corrected by more realistic exchange rates. In the meantime, trade talks can help avoid an outburst of destructive protection.[21] Three features would make the talks enticing, both to Congress and to the wider US business and farming communities.

First, the agenda for multilateral talks should give prominence to services, intellectual property, high technology products, and agriculture. These are areas of US export strength and the US government needs the enthusiastic support of its export constituencies to embark on new talks.

19. Stephen Marris, *Deficits and the Dollar: The World Economy at Risk,* POLICY ANALYSES IN INTERNATIONAL ECONOMICS (Washington: Institute for International Economics, forthcoming 1985).

20. This estimate assumes that US GNP in 1985 is about $4,000 billion and that the traded-goods sector amounts to $1,000 billion. The implied price ''pass-through'' coefficient of about 0.3 (10 percent divided by 35 percent) lies at the lower end of customary estimates.

21. In his address before the National Press Club on 25 April, 1985, Sen. John C. Danforth, the Chairman of the Senate Finance Subcommittee on International Trade, warned that Congress is unlikely to implement new trade liberalizing measures until a dollar correction has occurred. Indeed, by July 1985, some three hundred pieces of protectionist legislation had been introduced in the Congress. See *Wall Street Journal,* 31 July 1985, p. 1.

Second, countries with strong current account positions should take the lead in implementing their concessions. Japan, in particular, should make advance concessions on nontariff barriers in areas such as telecommunications, semiconductors, pharmaceuticals, and wood and paper products. Japan could initially extend such concessions for a limited period, say five years, by which time the United States and other countries would either implement their own concessions or Japan could withdraw its concessions.

Third, the fairness strategy should be emphasized. This strategy translates into more discipline on subsidies (particularly on agricultural exports), a code on commercial counterfeiting, minimal standards in the workplace, and, over a period of time, reciprocal concessions from the newly industrializing countries (NICs) which maintain exceedingly high import barriers. The "level playing field" is a powerful metaphor for trade policy in the US Congress and the business community.

Trade talks involve more than wish lists. The United States must also accommodate foreign concerns in order to launch the Growth Round.

First, the United States could agree to negotiate on two central topics: major reforms in the world monetary system and significant expansion of development finance. A new monetary system would reduce misalignment and volatility of exchange rates. An expansion of development finance could promote trade liberalization by developing countries.

Second, the United States could table a model plan for the self-financed adjustment of troubled industries and agriculture. The plan would provide for tariffs or auctioned quotas for the temporary protection of industries in distress, the dedication of revenues to downsizing those industries, and the gradual liberalization of trade. This approach would enable the United States to negotiate meaningful liberalization in difficult areas such as textiles and apparel, dairy, and steel, provided other countries were likewise prepared to downsize and liberalize their troubled industries.

Third, the United States could take a much more moderate view on export controls imposed for national security and foreign policy reasons. Even with the end of the pipeline sanctions, export controls remain a major irritant to relations with Europe. The United States could improve the atmosphere by agreeing to limit national security controls to items of immediate military significance that are not available from third countries. The United States could also concede that, once goods and technology enter international commerce, they will not be subject to retroactive controls.

TABLE 2.1   **Growth of output and employment (average annual percentage rate)**

	1970–80		1980–84	
	United States	*European Community*	*United States*	*European Community*
GDP growth	2.9	2.9	2.0	0.8
Employment growth	2.0	0.2	0.8	−0.6

Source: European Economy, November 1984.

THE EUROPEAN COMMUNITY

The number one European priority is jobs. Table 2.1 shows that, in the decade between 1970 and 1980, output growth in Europe was about the same as in the United States, but employment growth in Europe was minuscule. In the period 1980–84, European output growth was very modest and employment actually shrank. Today European unemployment remains extremely high, at rates exceeding 10 percent in many countries.

The purpose of trade liberalization is to make growth possible by increasing efficiency. Liberalization encourages domestic structural reforms which, when coupled with appropriate domestic demand policies, can stimulate employment growth.[22] In the European context, employment growth requires two conditions: an end to national legislation that mandates high wage costs and inhibits layoffs and a strong dose of demand stimulation. Trade policy is not the main vehicle for these reforms, but good trade policy can make it easier to take the necessary steps.

For example, the European Community remains far from the integrated economic unit envisaged by its founding fathers almost 30 years ago. National customs and technical standards badly inhibit the free flow of goods and services within the European Community.[23] Progress toward a real common market in Europe requires far greater movement of labor, capital, and goods.

---

22. This point was recently made by R.J. Wonnacott, *Canada/United States Free Trade: Problems and Opportunities* (Toronto: Ontario Economic Council, 1985).

23. One estimate puts the cost due merely to border delays in intra-EC trade at $10 billion a year. See *The Economist,* 24 November 1984, p. 13.

This is recognized by European leaders, who are pushing the concept of "Citizens Europe," designed to allow citizens to travel through the whole of Europe with fewer border checks.

The lack of standardization in the European market effectively restrains the development of new high technology industries. This problem is most apparent in the telecommunications and information technology sectors where fragmented and cartelized markets foster redundant R&D programs and high product costs.

Meanwhile, the common agricultural policy (CAP) has become an economic burden on the European Community. The CAP now accounts for about 75 percent of the EC budget. A fall in the foreign exchange value of the dollar would trigger further large increases in EC restitution payments.[24] In the short run, Europe could deal with its fiscal problem by raising the value-added tax. But at some point, EC-member governments may tire of allowing the agricultural sector to make huge calls on common resources. Individual Europeans might instead enjoy a tax cut; other sectors might better profit from EC-wide programs.

How can new trade negotiations help? More liberal trade policies can permit more demand stimulation without the specter of inflation. Beyond that, trade talks can spur cooperative action within the European Community. The negotiation of the Government Procurement Code during the Tokyo Round provides an instructive precedent. Pressure to develop joint positions for the GATT talks in Geneva helped break the deadlock that had prevented agreement on an *internal* directive on procurement policies. Right now, progress is being made to forge EC-wide policies on trade in services. In short, external talks provide Brussels a stronger mandate to carry out internal rationalization.

A trade negotiation can also help downsize—not dismantle—the CAP, buy out growing rights, and systematically retire high-cost land from production. These steps would make a very significant contribution to European efficiency.

Trade negotiations can also yield important new export opportunities for

---

24. According to a member of the European Parliament, each 1 percent decline in the value of the dollar against the ECU would cost the European Community about $70 million for additional export subsidies. See David M. Curry, "Farm Policy is Fundamental to E.C.," *Europe* (July/August 1985), p. 37.

European firms. European businessmen are highly impatient with the one-way street in trade relations with successful developing countries, that is, the "easy" access to Europe as against the "hard" access to South Korea, Brazil, India, and other LDC markets. Joint US-EC-Japanese pressure could help persuade those countries that reciprocal concessions are a good idea. In addition, EC trade prospects with heavily indebted LDCs would be enhanced if significant World Bank and IMF funds are made available contingent on basic trade reforms. To this end, the European Community could push the United States and Japan to increase their contribution to the international financial institutions in the context of LDC participation in new trade talks.

Like the United States, Europe has pressed Japan to liberalize trade in areas that would benefit EC exporters, for example, on such items as luxury automobiles, high quality textiles, spirits and tobacco products, and selected services, such as insurance, finance, and management consulting.[25] Indeed, for the European Community to liberalize many of its QRs, which are largely directed against Japanese imports, Japan would have to provide significant and reciprocal concessions in areas of interest to EC exporters.

The European Community needs to reach a lasting accommodation with the United States on two important sources of trade friction: steel and agriculture. Both problems involve the question of permissible subsidies. Here the dimensions of the trade-off seem clear: the United States could concede the legitimacy of adjustment subsidies used for downsizing the steel industry and other troubled sectors (including agriculture, if subsidies are used to retire land from commercial production); while Europe, the United States, and other countries could gradually limit the use of agricultural subsidies that encourage excess production and exports.

JAPAN

In recent years, Japan has successfully pursued a policy of export-led growth and amassed huge trade surpluses with most of its major partners. After recovering from the second oil shock by the end of 1980, Japan's cumulative current account surplus exploded: from $4.8 billion (1981), to $6.9 billion

---

25. The EC ran an average surplus with Japan on services of almost 2 billion ECU per year from 1979 to 1982, while its merchandise trade was in deficit by more than 8 billion ECU. The figures are from *Eurostat*, as cited in the 1984 EC submission to the GATT on trade in services.

(1982), to $20.8 billion (1983), to $35 billion (1984), to perhaps $45 billion (1985), a five-year total exceeding $110 billion. These surpluses are not the outcome of a new wave of Japanese protection. Instead, they reflect a high Japanese savings rate, a conservative fiscal deficit (under 3 percent of GNP in 1984, down from 5 percent to 6 percent of GNP in 1980), and an open world market that permits internal stringency to be translated into external surpluses.[26]

As befits the sweepstakes winner in the world trade race, Japan helped orchestrate the Bonn Summit call for a new round of trade negotiations. But Japanese interest in a new round does not translate into Japanese eagerness for rapid progress. Japan has no bilateral agenda. Bolstered by a competitive yen[27] and by high product quality, Japanese exporters can easily gain access to world markets. In fact, Japanese companies "voluntarily" restrain their exports over a broad range of manufactured goods, for example, autos, steel, and consumer electronics in Europe, and autos and steel in the United States. *Not* having specific demands of the United States and Europe means that Japan need not be aggressive in pursuing negotiations. In fact, Japan's main goal is to avoid a protectionist backlash. Japan has more to gain from the negotiating process than from the actual conclusion of agreements—agreements that would likely require Japan to make substantial concessions.

Japanese priorities for a new round were spelled out in a paper circulated in Geneva for the November 1984 meeting of the GATT contracting parties:

- reverse the erosion of discipline of the GATT system, with a particular focus on the issue of safeguards

- improve trade prospects for the debt-ridden LDCs

- reform the GATT to meet the trade challenges of the 1980s and 1990s, including reforms of GATT dispute settlement procedures and increased participation by LDCs in the GATT codes negotiated during the Tokyo Round.

---

26. For an analysis of the macroeconomic issues, see C. Fred Bergsten and William R. Cline, *The United States–Japan Economic Problem*, POLICY ANALYSES IN INTERNATIONAL ECONOMICS (Washington: Institute for International Economics, forthcoming 1985).

27. As noted in chapter 1, the yen is substantially undervalued against the US dollar; it has, however, *appreciated* somewhat on a trade-weighted basis since 1982.

This agenda addresses important systemic problems. But none of the issues requires Japan to make significant concessions. Other countries are unlikely to let Japan off so easily. The United States has exerted noisy pressure on Japan in the wake of a mounting bilateral trade deficit (about $37 billion in 1984, perhaps reaching $45 billion in 1985). The European Community and the Association of Southeast Asian Nations (ASEAN) have joined the queue demanding better access to the Japanese market. Protests from ASEAN leaders have been especially bitter. Like Japan before them, the ASEAN countries have adopted policies of export-led growth. But in recent years, Japan has not increased its purchases from ASEAN countries, even though the yen has appreciated sharply against other currencies in the region.[28] From a Pacific Basin perspective, Japanese trade barriers are the number one trade problem; unless this problem is addressed, trade talks have little meaning for those countries.

Indeed, many government and business leaders in the United States and Europe believe the "Japan problem" is the key issue on the trade agenda. Opening the Japanese market to imports and redressing Japan's burgeoning trade and current account surpluses are regarded as the sine qua non for successful negotiations. Without progress towards these goals, the implementation of multilateral trade reforms will be difficult, if not impossible.

Obviously trade liberalization is not the whole answer to Japan's current account surplus. Tax cuts, higher spending, and appreciation of the yen are critical, but trade liberalization plays more than a minor role in the drama.

First, Japan has both an opportunity and a responsibility to show the world that huge current account surpluses can be harnessed to the cause of trade liberalization. As Willy de Clercq puts it, Japan should display a sense of noblesse oblige to match its economic power. In April 1985, a leading Japanese official, Kiichi Miyazawa, suggested that Japan should offer a "down payment" for a new round by cutting tariffs by 25 percent and offering to eliminate them entirely during the negotiations. In June 1985, Japan did in fact cut tariffs on most products by 20 percent.[29]

Second, the trade that might flow from *complete* liberalization by Japan is

---

28. *The Economist,* 19 January 1985, p. 67.

29. Kiichi Miyazawa, "A Reflection on the Present Challenges," (Paper presented to the Trilateral Commission, Tokyo, 21 April 1985), p. 5. See also *Washington Post,* 26 June 1985, p. D1.

T A B L E 2.2 **Guesstimates of increased Japanese imports from complete liberalization of government trade barriers and buy-national procurement practices of Japanese firms (billion dollars)**

	Increased Japanese imports
Agricultural and natural resource goods from United States	
Rice[a]	1.0
Beef	0.3
Citrus and vegetables	0.2
Logs and lumber	1.0
Fish	0.4
Coal	1.0
Subtotal, agricultural goods and natural resources	3.9
Manufactured goods from United States	
Cigarettes[b]	1.9
Pulp and paper	0.5
Electronic components and computers	1.0
Telecommunications	0.7
Chemicals, pharmaceuticals, cosmetics	1.5
Medical equipment	0.4
All other manufactured goods	0.3
Subtotal, manufactured goods	6.3
Insurance, brokerage, mutual funds	0.3
Total increase in Japanese imports from United States	10.5
Increase in Japanese imports from third countries[c]	11.8
Total increase in imports[d]	22.3

Source: Based on interviews with trade associations and other observers of US-Japanese trade.

a. Self-sufficiency in rice is regarded as a matter of national survival by many Japanese. Thus, it is highly unlikely that Japan will significantly liberalize rice imports in the foreseeable future. The estimate here assumes that, if Japan did liberalize, imports would provide about 9.0 million metric tons out of consumption of about 13.0 million tons, and that the United States would supply about 30 percent of the imports.

b. An increase in Japanese cigarette imports would reduce Japanese tobacco imports. Tobacco represents a modest fraction (under 25 percent) of the wholesale price of cigarettes, however; Japanese cigarettes are made half from Japanese tobacco, while US cigarettes are made almost entirely from US tobacco.

c. The United States supplies about 40 percent of Japan's food imports and about 40 percent of Japan's manufactured imports. The figure here assumes that third-country suppliers increase their exports to Japan by only three-quarters as much as the United States relative to their base levels of trade.

d. A preliminary cross-country regression of imports against GNP indicates that the Japanese import share is 2.8 percent less than the predicted coefficient for a country of Japan's size. The 2.8 percent deviation is not statistically significant. In 1983 GNP, however, 2.8 percent would translate into an additional $32 billion of imports. See C. Fred Bergsten and William R. Cline, *The United States–Japan Economic Problem,* POLICY ANALYSES IN INTERNATIONAL ECONOMICS (Washington: Institute for International Economics, forthcoming 1985).

not trivial. Complete liberalization would require not only an end to government-inspired barriers, but also the establishment of meaningful antitrust procedures so that importers could challenge the buying decisions of Japanese firms that are linked, through cross-ownership ties, to a network of domestic suppliers (the *keiretsu* system). Guesstimates of the import consequences of complete liberalization, shown in table 2.2, suggest that total Japanese imports might increase by more than $22 billion. Liberalization of this scope would of course require years, not months, to achieve. An increase in Japanese imports of this magnitude would have macroeconomic consequences. It would depress the exchange value of the yen and thereby increase Japanese exports, perhaps leaving little *net* change in Japan's trade balance. But liberalization might also reduce Japanese business savings by depressing profits (or creating losses) in protected industries such as paper, petrochemicals, and cigarettes. A reduction in business savings would correspondingly reduce Japan's demand for foreign financial assets and thereby curtail Japan's current account surplus.

For Japan, the preservation of a liberal system would be its own reward. Japan probably would avert a new wave of barriers on telecommunications, pharmaceuticals, and other products. Moreover, Japan could then demand that foreign barriers against imports of automobiles, consumer electronics, and a range of other goods be terminated as Japan's current account surplus diminishes.

DEVELOPING COUNTRIES

Most LDCs have exhibited little enthusiasm for new trade negotiations. Like other countries, they are disappointed both by the results of the Tokyo Round, in particular the failure to reach agreement on a safeguards code, and by the erosion of the world trading system resulting from protective measures in textiles, apparel, steel, and selected agricultural products.

The LDCs are not a coherent bloc with unified trade policies and objectives. Some, such as Mexico, are commercially integrated into the world trading system, even if they stand apart in their institutional arrangements. Others, such as Chad and Burma, lie outside the mainstream of international commerce.

Only a few developing countries are likely to participate, even if reluctantly, in the negotiating process. The vast majority of LDCs will be more interested in parallel negotiations on development finance and debt than in trade talks.

TABLE 2.3 **Key LDC participants in the Growth Round**

Countries	1983 Trade (billion dollars)	
	Exports	Imports
Heavily indebted LDCs		
Argentina	7.8	4.5
Brazil	21.9	16.8
Colombia	3.0	5.0
Indonesia	21.2	16.4
Jamaica	0.7	1.4
Mexico[a]	21.1	8.2
Philippines	4.9	8.2
Yugoslavia	9.9	12.2
More creditworthy LDCs		
Algeria[a]	11.2	10.3
China[a]	22.2	21.3
Egypt	3.1	10.0
Hong Kong[a]	22.0	24.0
India	8.5	13.3
Malaysia	14.1	13.2
Singapore	21.8	28.2
South Korea	24.5	26.9

Source: GATT, *International Trade 1983/84*, table A5.
a. Countries that are *not* contracting parties to the GATT.

The prospective active participants, listed in table 2.3, divide into two groups: heavily indebted nations and more creditworthy LDCs.

Excluded from the list of active participants are the Eastern European countries and a great many smaller LDCs. Most oil-exporting countries—for which trade concessions on general merchandise and services are of lesser interest—are also omitted from the list, although problems in the petrochemical sector may prompt the participation of Saudi Arabia, which now maintains observer status in the GATT.

Brazil and India, the two most active LDC participants in the Tokyo Round, have been the most vocal opponents of launching a new round. Their concerns are twofold: they see little evidence that OECD countries will commit themselves to significant trade liberalization in LDC sectors of comparative advantage, such as textiles and steel; and they hesitate to negotiate more liberal rules for services trade in the face of strong political opposition from their own highly protected firms. These concerns need to be addressed, but they are not of overriding importance. Both Brazil and India have higher priorities: Brazil's first and foremost concern is to resolve its debt burden, while India seeks to modernize its industrial sector, including high technology industries, through increased trade and foreign investment. A further erosion of the multilateral trading system would complicate these tasks, while both objectives could be advanced in a new trade round.

Of particular interest will be the participation of Mexico and China. Mexico is a leading LDC exporter and was quite active in the Tokyo Round negotiations. Despite Mexico's stated willingness to consider participation in the Growth Round,[30] perceptions of Mexico's future role are clouded by its rejection of GATT membership in 1979. Mexico has, however, embarked in the past few years on an ambitious program of trade liberalization and conversion of nontariff barriers to tariff barriers. The recent conclusion of a Mexico-US bilateral agreement on subsidies and countervailing duties may facilitate Mexican participation in the Subsidies Code and could lead Mexico to reexamine its skeptical attitude toward the GATT.

Meanwhile, China is actively seeking a place in the GATT. China plays a key role in negotiations on textiles and apparel. The potentially vast Chinese market holds considerable fascination for developed and developing countries alike. A recent study by the World Bank, however, projects that Chinese spending for food, clothing, and consumer durables will grow by only 4 percent to 7 percent annually through the year 2000.[31] In the near term, the world trading community will be more concerned with China as an export competitor than as an import market.

The 15 years from 1965 to 1980 were golden years for many LDCs. The LDC share of world exports in manufactures almost doubled from 1965 to 1980 (from 5.5 percent to 9.7 percent), while the LDC share of world exports of primary products increased by a third (from 40 percent to 54 percent). The advanced developing countries of Southeast Asia conspicuously shifted from a reliance on primary products to a reliance on manufacturing. In the process, some of them, such as South Korea and Singapore, became major players in the world market.

---

30. Statement by President Miguel de la Madrid to the Mexico–US Business Committee, 11 February 1985, *Mexico Today*, vol. 3 (February 1985), p. 6.

31. Jacques van der Gaag, "Private Household Consumption in China: A Study of People's Livelihood," World Bank Staff Working Paper, no. 701. Cited in *The Economist*, 11 May 1985, p. 82.

But most LDCs were badly buffeted by the second oil shock of 1979, the subsequent global recession, high interest rates, and a sharp drop in commodity prices. Since the Tokyo Round, their exports have faced increasing barriers in developed country markets, especially for steel, textiles and apparel, footwear, and consumer electronics.

For many of these countries, especially those in Latin America, the principal problem is debt. International indebtedness to private banks reached approximately $750 billion in 1982, of which 80 percent was owed by the developing countries. Many nations, like Argentina and the Philippines, face bleak prospects of paying even the interest. Several countries, such as Mexico, Brazil, Argentina, and Peru, have been forced to reschedule their loans.

Declining earnings and debt servicing difficulties make it difficult for LDCs to buy imports. This problem should concern the industrialized world because, up to 1980, the LDCs were a major market for the developed countries. In 1973, 37 percent of Japanese exports, 29 percent of US exports, and 28 percent of EC exports went to the LDCs. By 1980, these shares had risen to 44 percent, 39 percent, and 38 percent, respectively. Thus, the decline of more than $50 billion in imports of 16 heavily indebted LDCs between 1981 and 1984 was widely felt by exporters in the developed world.[32]

What is the strategy from here? First and foremost, LDCs need to return to the brisk growth rates they enjoyed in the 1960s and the 1970s. All LDCs need a strong global macroeconomic climate. In addition, in most cases, growth will have to be export-led and internationally financed. The indebted LDCs need more resources from the World Bank and the IMF, and the creditworthy NICs need a more open world economy.

The overriding objective of all LDCs in the Growth Round is the maintenance and strengthening of the multilateral trading system. An improved safeguards system and the liberalization of existing QRs will improve LDC access to OECD markets. For example, LDCs are more likely to wrest concessions on textile and apparel quotas in the context of a new trade round. As part of the overall liberalization process, progress should also be made to reduce the extent of tariff escalation.

The creditworthy NICs have the most to gain from new trade talks because they have the most to lose if possibilities for export-led growth are foreclosed.

---

32. GATT, *International Trade 1983/84* (Geneva, 1984), table A29; and IMF, *Directions of Trade Statistics.*

Pure self-interest, plus a little pressure from other LDCs, should prompt the creditworthy NICs to accept the principle that they must pay in concessions granted for concessions received.

What concessions are LDCs likely to be called on to make? First, much more should be sought from the NICs than from the other LDCs. Second, the pace of liberalization should be phased according to the level of development and the balance of payments circumstances of each country.

Concessions from the NICs could take the form of conversion of QRs to tariffs, followed by the reduction of absurdly high tariffs (those over 100 percent) and, if necessary, accompanied by devaluation. In addition, the NICs could extensively bind tariffs, reduce trade-related investment restrictions, dismantle countertrade requirements, adopt a standstill on new restrictions on transborder data flows, and graduate from the special provisions of Part IV of the GATT.[33] In practice, graduation will mean that NICs cannot pull back bound tariff concessions without paying compensation to affected exporting countries. Concessions of this nature may seem painful to Brazil, India, Mexico, Korea, and other successful NICs, but such discipline will ensure that industries in these countries adjust to foreign competition—actions that are likely to promote growth just as much as improved access to western markets.

THE SMALLER INDUSTRIAL COUNTRIES

In many ways, it is artificial to discuss smaller developed countries together. Canada, Sweden, Norway, Finland, Switzerland, and Australia have diverse industries in both manufacturing and resource-based primary sectors. Canada, Sweden, and Switzerland have internationally competitive high technology and service industries; Canada and Australia are major agricultural exporters; Canada and Finland are major exporters of wood products; Canada and Norway are major producers and exporters of oil and gas.

While their economic interests are diverse, their trade is dominated by the large markets of their close neighbors. These countries have a common

---

33. Part IV is the vehicle for exceptional import restrictions, access to the generalized system of preferences (GSP) and other special measures. Part IV might better be reserved for the least developed countries. Even those countries might be asked to make a showing, by a preponderance of the evidence, that infant industry trade barriers would further development before imposing such barriers.

TABLE 2.4   **Export markets of Canada, the Nordics, Switzerland, and Australia (billion dollars and percentage, 1983)**

Country	Total exports	To United States	To European Community	To Japan
Canada	$76.7	$53.9	$5.5	$3.9
	(100.0)	(70.0)	(7.2)	(5.1)
Nordics[a]	$57.9	$3.7	$30.4	$0.7
	(100.0)	(6.4)	(52.5)	(1.3)
Switzerland	$25.6	$2.2	$12.6	$0.7
	(100.0)	(8.6)	(49.2)	(2.7)
Australia	$20.7	$2.1	$3.0	$5.7
	(100.0)	(10.1)	(14.5)	(27.5)

Source: IMF, *Directions of Trade Yearbook 1984.*
a. Sweden, Norway, and Finland.

disadvantage: their small home markets make it difficult for them to maintain a high degree of international competitiveness. Moreover, their export markets are highly concentrated geographically. As shown in table 2.4, Canada depends on the United States for more than 70 percent of its export earnings; the Nordics and Switzerland depend on the European Community for 50 percent of their exports. Australia is more diversified, with a little more than a quarter of its exports going to Japan and another quarter going to the United States and the European Community together.

For Canada, the Nordics, and Switzerland, the central question is improved and more secure access to the markets of their larger neighbors. Canada, the Nordics, and Switzerland thus have important bilateral agendas with the United States and the European Community, respectively. Australia (like New Zealand) has an overriding interest in liberal treatment for agricultural and mineral exports; the Australian agenda necessarily encompasses the United States, Europe, and Japan.

Canada

Since 1982, more than half of the growth in Canadian GNP has been associated with an increase in exports to the United States. The United States now takes more than 70 percent of total Canadian exports. Canada's first priority is to ensure that the US market remains open to Canadian goods and services. Even though 80 percent of Canadian exports already enter the United States duty free, numerous barriers remain, including high tariffs on particular products, a range of domestic subsidies, and restrictive government procurement practices.[34]

Sectors of particular interest to Canada include urban mass transportation equipment, telecommunications, power-generating equipment, electric power, petrochemicals, and wood and paper products. In return, Canadian concessions are likely to focus on sectors of interest to the United States such as dairy and wheat, high technology goods and services, and trade-related investment and intellectual property issues.

Canada should proceed on a bilateral track to ensure that specific problems in US-Canada trade are covered. Canada also needs, however, to pursue export opportunities in new or expanding markets in the Pacific Basin, especially in resource-based industries such as forest products.

While supporting a new GATT trade round, Canada is also exploring the option of a free trade area with the United States, implemented in stages over a long period of time. A Canadian-US free trade area could serve as one of the building blocks, like the European Community and European Free Trade Association (EFTA), of a wider industrial free trade area after the year 2000.

The Nordics and Switzerland

More than half of the exports from Sweden, Norway, and Finland go to the European Community; the share of Nordic exports to all European countries is comparable to the share of Canada's exports to the United States. Approximately the same statistics apply to Switzerland. As with Canada, the primary goal for Switzerland and the Nordics is to seek open access to their largest foreign market. Swiss and Nordic trade with Europe is inhibited by a vast array of subsidies, standards, and procurement restrictions. The barriers are particularly cumbersome because in many respects the European Community is not a common market; indeed, in telecommunications and other high technology sectors, the EC market is highly fragmented.

---

34. Exports of both countries are inhibited by the restrictive procurement policies of states and provinces, whose practices are not subject to the GATT Government Procurement Code.

Sweden and Switzerland are particularly sensitive to restrictions—especially export controls on access to new technologies in electronics, telecommunications, and robotics. Large markets are needed to afford economies of scale in production and to recoup massive R&D costs over a short period of time. To stay abreast, these countries would benefit from multilateral rules: (1) to discipline extraterritorial national controls, often enacted and enforced in the overly broad search for national security, and perhaps masking protectionist intentions; (2) to promote national treatment and establishment rights, which would help further the activities of Swedish and Swiss firms in foreign markets; and (3) to extend GATT rules to cover trade in services, particularly banking, insurance, and telecommunications services.

A major Nordic strategy, within the larger multilateral talks, will involve closer EFTA-EC trade. Like a Canadian-US free trade area, a closer EFTA-EC arrangement could serve as a building block of a wider industrial free trade area after the year 2000.

Many of the concessions that the Nordic countries and Switzerland would be called on to make would fall in the agricultural area. Swiss agriculture is even more protected than EC agriculture;[35] indeed, some observers have likened the Swiss countryside to a sheltered garden. The same can be said of vegetables and specialty crops in Sweden. Another important area of Swiss protection is textiles and apparel; to a lesser extent, Sweden and Norway also continue to protect their own textile and apparel industries. In short, these highly successful trading countries still have valuable bargaining chips to play in the Growth Round.

Australia

More than three-quarters of Australian exports are foodstuffs, raw materials, and fuels. Not surprisingly, Australia is vitally interested in the improvement of GATT rules for agriculture and in the effective enforcement of those rules. Australia (along with New Zealand) has been frustrated in previous negotiations and dissatisfied with GATT rulings on European sugar subsidies and other agricultural questions. Moreover, Australia has been the unintended victim of various bilateral agreements on agricultural products. For example,

---

35. *Financial Times*, 1 August 1985, p. 4. According to some studies, Swiss farm subsidies total between SF 3 billion and SF 5 billion a year.

after the United States and Japan "liberalized" bilateral trade in beef, Australian exporters confronted lower import quotas in the Japanese market.

With its efficient agricultural sector, Australia would have much to gain from the freer play of market forces. Thus, Australia would be a leading beneficiary of a US-EC agreement to reduce agricultural export subsidies and an international commitment to promote adjustment and respect the safeguard principles of Article XIX.[36]

Unlike Canada and the Nordics, Australia does not have a predominant trading partner. Nevertheless, both Australia and New Zealand (which have their own free trade area) may decide to explore a larger free trade arrangement with the United States. Again this could serve as a building block for a wider industrial free trade area after the year 2000.

In the meantime, Australia and New Zealand should not ignore bilateral ties with their Southeast Asian neighbors. This is the most dynamic growth region in the world today, and nearly 20 percent of Australian exports already go to the Southeast Asian area. The major concession that Australia and New Zealand can make to the ASEAN region, and indeed to the world trading system as a whole, is to lower and to bind tariffs on a wide range of manufactured goods.

---

36. Andrew Farran, "New GATT Round Vital to Australia," *The Australian Financial Review*, 22 April 1985, p. 20.

3 The Negotiating Package

The negotiating package assembled here represents a "critical mass" of key issues. For each issue, we summarize the central problems and provide a strategy for addressing them, giving due regard to political constraints. This short monograph does not offer a complete menu; many other issues will undoubtedly arise in the course of trade talks. But it proposes a set of priority goals for the talks, which could provide the needed impetus both to get them going and to drive them to a successful conclusion.

The package is organized around the seven strategic goals outlined in chapter 2:

- a meaningful standstill against new protection

- an extension of GATT principles to cover new areas

- the replacement of quantitative restrictions (QRs) by auctioned quotas or tariffs with dedication of the resulting revenue to industry adjustment

- the satisfaction of demand growth for the products of troubled industries by the most competitive supplier

- the extension of fair trade principles to cover new areas of abuse

- the use of a conditional most-favored-nation (MFN) approach

- the implementation of concessions on schedules that reflect current account surpluses and deficits.

Safeguards and Adjustment

The new round will have to deal with two parallel problems: how to liberalize entrenched trade barriers, and how to ensure that future barriers are both

41

temporary and degressive. Both will require a reexamination of the GATT safeguard rules.

Prior trade rounds reduced most of the high tariffs erected in the 1930s, thereby eliminating much of the "water" from the system of protection in OECD countries. Left now are high tariffs and hard-core QRs that protect distressed sectors such as textiles, steel, and footwear, plus new "voluntary" restraints that, in recent years, have been substituted for more visible means of protection. The high protective barriers that are found today in OECD countries principally serve to safeguard troubled industries from the pressures of world competition.

Article XIX of the General Agreement on Tariffs and Trade (GATT) contains a safeguards system that was meant to provide the basic framework for affording troubled industries temporary relief from import competition, through protection implemented on an even-handed basis against *all* foreign suppliers. The rules of Article XIX have usually *not* been observed, however. The United States, Canada, and Australia have been virtually the only countries to invoke Article XIX, and even they protect a great many industries outside the GATT framework through various means of "special protection"—voluntary restraint agreements (VRAs), orderly marketing agreements (OMAs),[1] and industry-to-industry understandings—that often persist for long periods of time and usually discriminate among foreign suppliers. Such measures distort comparative advantage both between importing and exporting countries and among exporting countries, and often divert export sales to third countries.

There are two basic causes for the virtual breakdown of the GATT safeguards system. First, domestic adjustment programs in most countries have been nonexistent or inadequate; second, it is easier to restrict trade from aggressive new entrants than from all participants. Liberalization of the international trading system largely depends on effective adjustment programs for troubled industries and a return to the principle that, when trade restraints are imposed, they bear equally on imports from all suppliers.

To help speed a return to the precepts of Article XIX, government-sponsored adjustment programs should offer temporary and degressive relief rather than indefinite protection at fixed levels. That relief should be limited in amount rather than open-ended, adjustment should foster contraction

---

1. VRAs and OMAs both are negotiated quota restrictions. The former is enforced by the exporting country; the latter by the importing country.

instead of revival, and the relief program should contain built-in sources of dedicated revenue.

Widespread experience indicates that, to regain their international competitiveness, troubled industries must downsize to a viable core.[2] The industry seeking protection should decide how this is to be done and submit its own proposals when applying for import relief.

Adjustment packages should neither require an infusion of public capital nor coerce investment from private firms. The latter approach was commended to the US steel industry by the Trade and Tariff Act of 1984,[3] but experience in Germany, Australia, and the United Kingdom suggests that forced investment programs have rarely borne out early expectations. New private investment should certainly not be discouraged from entering troubled industries, but the entry of new capital should neither anticipate nor justify indefinite protection from foreign competition.

Experience also suggests that restraints, unless prohibitive, are unlikely to do more than slow the pace of import growth. In fact, troubled industries will usually have to shed labor as they cut costs and improve productivity, regardless of import relief.

Building on this body of experience, new GATT safeguard rules should pursue two parallel tracks, one to facilitate orderly adjustment for new industries seeking relief and another to dismantle existing schemes of protection.

ORDERLY ADJUSTMENT IN NEW CASES

Domestic adjustment programs must provide the centerpiece for national accommodation to the realities of the international marketplace. This principle is central to all else. The role of import relief in adjustment schemes should at most be limited to the provision of "temporary breathing space."

The obstacles to reducing and terminating relief are pronounced when QRs

---

2. Gary Clyde Hufbauer and Howard F. Rosen, *Trade Policy for Troubled Industries*, POLICY ANALYSES IN INTERNATIONAL ECONOMICS (Washington: Institute for International Economics, forthcoming 1985).

3. Section 806 requires the major US steel companies as a group to commit "substantially all of their net cash flow from steel product operations for purposes of reinvestment in, and modernization of, that industry. . . ."

are the chosen tool. QRs can be made infinitely complex, masking their actual costs both to government officials and to consumers. Moreover, QRs establish incentives for their perpetuation, both on the part of the domestic industry and on the part of exporters lucky enough to hold quota rights.[4] The profits of Toyota and Nissan, as well as of General Motors, Ford, and Chrysler, ballooned from the sharply higher prices paid by US consumers as a result of the US-Japan VRA on autos.[5]

Countries should commit themselves to avoid QRs in all forms, including "voluntary" agreements. Instead, tariffs should be the preferred means of implementing new safeguard measures. Where tariffs are not practical, auctioned quotas would be the second best approach.[6] Tariffs and auctioned quotas are more transparent and easier to adjust in a downward direction. They allow imports to come from the cheapest source, and they provide a source of revenue that can be dedicated for worker and firm adjustment

---

4. Another problem with QRs is their effect on the trade of third countries. Selective protection puts a cloud over the trade of all countries, because restraints are only viable if other foreign suppliers do not increase their exports to fill the void. The unstable dynamic of selective protection often leads to an extension of controls to cover imports from other countries, as happened recently with US-EC steel quotas.

5. The influence of "voluntary" trade quotas on corporate profits, as well as on harmonious international trading relations, was not lost on the Japanese. Following the expiration of formal restrictions in March 1985, the Ministry of International Trade and Industry (MITI) announced a plan for truly voluntary export restraints to limit sales to the United States to 2.3 million cars in 1985. *The Economist,* 4 May 1985, p. 76.

6. There is a great deal of difference between auctioned quotas and a tariff even when the auction rate initially turns out to be the same as the tariff rate: a quota system encourages high unit-value imports and discriminates against low unit-value imports (though this effect can be offset by providing different quotas for low unit-value and high unit-value items, or by requiring auction bids to be expressed in terms of a percentage of CIF value); a quota system insulates the domestic market from foreign supply and demand fluctuations; and a quota system takes away the discipline of a larger foreign market share. For all these reasons, most economists prefer a tariff to an auctioned quota. Public officials, however, greatly favor the implementation of protection through quotas assigned to foreign suppliers, rather than through auctioned quotas or tariffs. Not surprisingly, most safeguard actions in recent years have taken the form of quotas. A system of quota auctions might serve as an intermediate step to tariffs. Quota auctions are now used by Australia and New Zealand for a range of manufactured imports. To be sure, quota auctions raise a number of technical difficulties, many of which were outlined by Stanley Nehmer, President of Economic Consulting Services, Inc., in an address to the DC Bar Association on 25 July 1985.

assistance programs. The adjustment programs should be designed so that they do not serve as a revolving door for new entrants to the beleaguered industry. This is an easier task for concentrated industries, like steel, than for industries with many small firms, like apparel. With a little bureaucratic ingenuity, however, it should be possible to avert the revolving door problem.[7]

In addition, for a revamped Article XIX to work, national laws should be written so as to make the safeguard route attractive relative to other trade relief options. For instance, under current US law, it is much easier to demonstrate injury due to unfair trade practices (dumping or subsidies) than it is to make a case for escape clause relief. Disparities of this sort would be reduced if the injury and causation standards that qualify an industry for import relief under Article XIX provisions were made less stringent. Such changes would provide an incentive for the "self-selection" of industries for adjustment programs, a benefit that would more than compensate for the easier access to *temporary* import relief.

Implementation and enforcement of these general principles should be undertaken through a new safeguards code that revives, in modified form, the concepts of compensation and retaliation. Countries would be excused from the obligation to pay trade compensation when they observed the letter of the new code. Otherwise they would be obligated to pay compensation or face the threat of retaliation.[8]

DISMANTLING OLD BARRIERS

Nations invariably hesitate to dismantle existing protection on a unilateral basis. In order to reduce trade barriers that protect troubled industries, the major nations will have to undertake adjustment commitments on a coordinated basis. These countries will need to: reach agreement on the industries covered;

---

7. Hufbauer and Rosen, *Trade Policy for Troubled Industries*, ch. 7.

8. This approach is suggested by John H. Jackson, "The Role of GATT in Monitoring Safeguards and Promoting Adjustment," in *Domestic Adjustment and International Trade*, edited by Gary Clyde Hufbauer and Howard F. Rosen (Washington: Institute for International Economics, forthcoming 1986). The purpose of waiving compensation and retaliation is to make the safeguard regime of a new code no more onerous to importing countries than the present system of VRAs and OMAs, which typically are designed to induce the exporting country to forego its compensation and retaliation rights.

establish time limits for phasing out restraints; convert existing QRs to tariffs or auctioned quotas; provide adequate public revenue for adjustment purposes;[9] and define legitimate adjustment techniques that will not be subject to charges of unfair subsidization.

The time limits for phasing out restraints could be expressed in terms of minimum and optional maximum exit rates for workers in the affected industry, and specified growth rates in the market share of imports (for example, not less than 1 percent nor, at the election of the importing country, more than 3 percent growth in each case). Beyond these basics, each country should be free to construct the program most appropriate to its particular situation. The GATT Secretariat could be given a role in designing and monitoring national adjustment programs similar to that of the International Monetary Fund (IMF) in debt negotiations.

Why would entrenched firms, which often hold a lock grip on public policy, agree to surrender domestic markets? It strains credulity to suppose that they will suddenly awaken to the teachings of David Ricardo on the blessings of comparative advantage. Appropriate adjustment assistance, however, would offer these companies the prospect of an easier transition to new business opportunities. Moreover, if *trade* liberalization in the importing countries is accompanied by *investment* liberalization in the exporting countries, many of the companies can survive by establishing offshore manufacturing facilities. Workers have an even greater incentive: in many cases, they face loss of employment because productivity growth exceeds demand expansion. Early retirement and retraining assistance, available to all workers (scaled to their experience in the industry), would provide meaningful compensation for trade liberalization.

To some extent, the gradual conversion of allocated quotas to tariffs or auctioned quotas would entail "negative foreign aid," in the sense that quota rents now enjoyed by less developed countries (LDCs) such as Hong Kong, India, or Brazil would flow to European finance ministries or to the US Treasury. Accordingly, many LDCs might object to surrendering a fractional part of their existing quotas each year. Some of the richer LDCs are not particularly deserving of windfall transfers through the harvest of quota rents.

---

9. In some circumstances, there may be an embarrassment of riches: the revenues generated by converting quotas to quota auctions may far exceed the adjustment needs of the industry. In such cases, disbursements should be limited to actual need, and surplus revenues should be committed to adjustment in other industries.

In any event, the efficient LDCs would benefit from more open export markets over a period of time. Moreover, the loss of quota rents would be partially offset, for those LDCs willing to embark on their own programs of trade liberalization, through augmented IMF or World Bank financing, as spelled out in chapter 1.

Agriculture

World agricultural trade has grown markedly over the past two decades. World exports of agricultural products averaged $283 billion annually during the period 1980–83, up from $121 billion in 1973, and accounted for 15 percent of total world trade.[10] These buoyant trade figures mask a remarkable amount of distortion, however. In Europe, almost all agricultural goods sell well above world prices. In the United States, sugar sells at five times the world price while dairy products are about twice the world price. In Japan, rice is four times the world price. These prices reflect widespread anxiety about levels of farm income, food security, and a deep unwillingness by GATT members to submit their domestic farm programs to international discipline. Indeed, at the Bonn Summit, France sought to exempt much of agricultural trade from new trade talks.

Where they exist at all, GATT rules on agriculture are riddled with loopholes. Nontariff barriers have not been reduced, export subsidies are commonplace, and agricultural products are frequently dumped on world markets. Interventionist farm programs are politically attractive, as evidenced by the many regimes that exist in the European Community (the entire common agricultural policy CAP), in Japan (rice, wheat, beef, citrus), and in the United States (tobacco, meat, sugar, dairy).

Unfortunately, the United States, Europe, and Japan are living with policies designed for a bygone age when governments could set domestic farm prices and incomes without severe budget consequences and with little regard for the world market.[11] Left to itself, the traditional approach to agricultural

---

10. GATT, *International Trade 1983/84*, t. A1. The unit value index of global agricultural trade increased 64 percent over this period.

11. D. Gale Johnson, "World Grain Trade Beyond 2000" (Ottawa: The Centennial Forum of the International Wheat Council, 28 June 1984), p. 15.

trade will lead to still worse trade abrasions in the 1980s and 1990s. There are three interrelated reasons for projecting this unhappy outcome: (1) biotechnology advances are likely to accentuate overproduction of major crops, which will lead to (2) severe fiscal pressures as governments seek to maintain farm income; which will devolve into (3) a search for off-budget solutions, especially import restraints and export incentives.

OVERPRODUCTION

Overproduction of major products such as wheat and feedgrains, dairy, and sugar lies at the root of most agricultural trade problems. These three products alone account for 28 percent of the value of world agricultural trade.[12]

Global production of wheat and feedgrains totaled 1,295 million metric tons (mmt) in 1984, up by almost a third since 1974. For most major producing countries (with the notable exception of China), consumption has not kept pace with the growth in output.[13] Excess production had to be traded, stored, or, to a limited extent, given away as food aid. The volume of trade in wheat and feedgrains grew by more than 60 percent in the last decade. At the same time, world grain stocks grew by about 66 percent to more than 190 mmt. Stocks accounted for 15 percent of global consumption in 1984, compared to 12 percent in 1974. The United States, which accounts for almost a quarter of global production, holds 84 mmt or 44 percent of world stocks (compared to only 23.5 percent in 1974); the European Community (EC) holds 22 mmt; even India has accumulated substantial stocks.[14]

The growth of mountainous surpluses has sparked a rash of agricultural trade disputes, particularly between the United States and Europe. For grains, sugar, and dairy products, the world market has become a virtual dumping

---

12. US International Trade Commission, *World Trade Flows in Major Agricultural Products,* pub. no. 1684, April 1985, p. 44.

13. Barbara Insel, "A World Awash in Grain," *Foreign Affairs,* vol. 63, no. 4 (Spring 1985), p. 895.

14. Insel, "A World Awash in Grain," pp. 899–900. Recent harvests have been so abundant that India has become a net exporter of wheat, with a domestic stockpile of almost 30 million metric tons. See also *The Economist,* 11 May 1985, pp. 82–83.

ground for agricultural surpluses encouraged by US and EC farm programs. Dumping in foreign markets is seen as a more expedient way of dealing with burgeoning farm surpluses than paying for storage in expensive domestic stockpiles or paying farmers not to produce in the first place.

The countries that gain from these policies are perennial importers; for grains and dairy products, the main beneficiaries are the Soviet Union and China. Together, the two Communist giants account for around a quarter of world imports of wheat and feedgrains.[15]

World grain surpluses would be little affected if the industrial countries addressed the tragic problems of the Sahel and other regions that face famine. The shortfall in the Sahel has been estimated at 3 mmt to 4 mmt or only 2 percent of world grain stocks. Drawing down stocks to meet these urgent needs would have little effect on world prices and on national farm budgets. At US export prices prevailing in March 1985, 4 mmt of wheat would cost less than $600 million. The key questions involve means of distribution and reallocation of aid budgets. These political issues fall outside the scope of the trading system.

BUDGET CONSTRAINTS AND EXPORT SUBSIDIES

Existing programs were never meant to finance the amber waves of surplus grain and other products that now swamp demand. The cost of domestic farm programs has grown dramatically in recent years.

Agriculture accounts for more than 75 percent of the total EC budget; in 1983, the EC CAP cost 15.5 billion ECUs (equal to $13.8 billion), up from 12.4 billion ECUs in 1982. Almost two-thirds of the CAP expenditures in 1983 went to dairy (30.3 percent), cereals (15.9 percent), sugar (9.2 percent), and meat (9.5 percent).[16]

The European Community barely averted a fiscal crisis in 1984 over CAP expenditures. The main reason the CAP did not break the EC budget was the strong dollar. A strong dollar means that higher priced EC production, denominated in weaker EC currencies, is more in line with world prices set in dollars. This, in turn, means that the European Community has to provide

---

15. Insel, "A World Awash in Grain," p. 895.

16. *The Economist*, 7 April 1984, p. 44.

smaller export subsidies to enable European farm exports to compete in world markets.

The European Community has taken small but important first steps to limit production, to reduce the nominal increase in guaranteed prices, and to phase out "monetary compensation" (designed to offset intra-EC exchange rate movements). For example, EC milk quotas are scheduled to decline from 103 million tons in 1983 to 98.4 million tons over the period 1985–88.[17]

US agricultural subsidies, a mixture of price supports, loans and loan guarantees, and export credits, averaged about $19 billion annually in 1981–83.[18] Net farm income averaged only $23 billion annually during this period,[19] demonstrating that the typical US farmer, like his European counterpart, depends heavily on the federal dole.

The Reagan administration encountered stiff congressional resistance to its plans to cut price supports and to reduce federal credit available to farmers over the next five years. Much more popular is the administration's new program of export subsidies to help US farmers meet subsidized foreign competition in third-country markets. This program is estimated to cost $2 billion in 1985–87.[20]

Farm programs in the United States, in Europe, and in Japan have spawned a two-tier price system, with domestic prices at a higher level and world market prices at a much lower level. Separation between the tiers is promoted by export subsidies and maintained with protectionist measures, be they variable levies as in Europe or quotas and fees as in the United States and Japan.[21]

The time seems ripe for reform: budgetary constraints are building; import protection has led, in some products, to absurdly high price levels and gross

---

17. *The Economist*, 7 April 1984, p. 41. The European Community already has encountered difficulty in enforcing the scheduled production decline, however.

18. Insel, "A World Awash in Grain," p. 900.

19. Council of Economic Advisers, *Economic Report of the President*, February 1985, p. 338.

20. *Washington Post*, 16 May 1985, p. A1.

21. "Governments have long since learned that you can intervene in domestic farm prices only if you intervene in exports and imports, unless you have very, very deep pockets." Johnson, "World Grain Trade," p. 15.

economic distortions; and export subsidies are becoming ever more trouble-some, especially in the European Community and in the United States.

NEW APPROACHES TO AGRICULTURE

Even though the time for action is at hand, a "best guess" forecast might well hold that nothing will be done to reform agricultural programs over the next decade because political concerns over farm income and food security are simply too great. But a "business as usual" approach would have dire consequences. National budgets would burst with the burden of farm programs. Milk lakes would grow into milk oceans. The construction of storage elevators would become a growth industry. Urban land prices in Japan would continue skyward, keeping housing scarce, as agricultural land remained in rice production; meanwhile, US farm land would stay depressed.[22] Part of the pressure would be diverted by highly visible export subsidies (the CAP) and part by less visible export subsidies (PL 480). The net result would be huge additional pressure on efficient agricultural suppliers such as Australia, New Zealand, Canada, Argentina, and the United States.

What can be done if this "best guess" forecast collapses from its own internal contradictions? Basically, producing countries can limit output, either through the price mechanism or by production controls. In either case, the driving political force for a new approach would *not* be to enhance economic efficiency but rather to control national budget outlays.

In economic terms, the best solution would entail the use of the price mechanism to rationalize production, for example, through lower support prices or smaller deficiency payments. Such measures would yield immediate budget dividends.[23]

There is robust political opposition to such an approach in Japan, Europe, and the United States, however. In mid-1985, the European Community was deadlocked over an attempt to reduce grain prices by 1.8 percent, while the US Congress blocked administration efforts to cut sharply into farm subsidy

22. Average US farmland values dropped 12 percent from April 1984 to April 1985; in major producing states, prices were off almost 30 percent. *New York Times*, 12 June 1985, p. A23.

23. See, for example, Fred H. Sanderson, "Obstacles to US Agricultural Exports: What Can We Do About Them?" (Statement before the House Committee on Agriculture, 4 April 1985).

programs. Moreover, this approach, if carried very far, would result in huge losses in the value of farm land, drive many small farmers out of business, and lead to further consolidation into larger and more efficient farms (possibly increasing production to boot).

To ease the burden of adjustment, governments could phase in lower support prices over several years, while providing farmers with direct income supplements. Income supplements would exacerbate budget pressures, however, while lower prices would lead, at least in the short run, to increased dumping of surpluses on world markets. In short, the price mechanism alone will not solve the *political* problems of agricultural production and trade.

As a politically feasible alternative, governments could either limit the extent of farm acreage (for example, though variants of the US payment-in-kind (PIK) program or through the outright purchase of agricultural land) or limit the quantity of production eligible for support under national farm programs. The idea behind acreage and production controls is to limit the volume of subsidized agricultural output. Variants of this approach are already in place for selected crops in the United States and in Europe. For example, in the United States, the volume of peanuts eligible for price supports is limited; "over allocation" peanuts must be sold at market prices.

Wider international application of this approach would entail two elements: each country would agree to a cap (degressive over time) on the amount of its farm output that could benefit from existing government programs;[24] and each country would commit itself to the principle that additional output would only be produced and marketed at world prices, without deficiency payments or other supports. Over time, the subsidized share of total production would gradually decline until international trade was largely conducted without subsidies. Meanwhile, as the relative volume of subsidized output declined, the difference between higher-tier domestic prices and lower-tier world prices would shrink.

As an immediate objective, international negotiations would seek to phase out, and eventually to prohibit, agricultural export subsidies. Grain subsidies,

---

24. At the outset, for example, farmers might receive allocations of support program eligibility equal, say, to 75 percent of their average production over the past three years. The remaining 25 percent eligibility quota should be auctioned. Quota rights should be transferable. Over time, governments would decrease the volume of output eligible for support, and an increasing share of the declining overall quota would be sold at auction. In this way, support programs would be phased out gradually, for example, over a generation of farmers, about twenty-five years.

for example, might be phased out over a five-year period. In addition, negotiations would seek to liberalize import restrictions, so that the growth, at least, in domestic demand was satisfied at world market prices. To the extent possible, import barriers would be administered by way of tariffs, auctioned quotas, or variable levies, rather than by assigned quotas, and the revenues would be devoted to defraying the costs of reducing farm acreage and farm livestock. Preliminary calculations for the United States suggest that revenues derived from auctioned quotas would more than absorb the costs of downsizing the sugar, dairy, and fishery industries.[25]

The combination of restraint on the size of agricultural programs and the gradual implementation of market principles would represent a radical departure from 40 years of farm policy—40 years dedicated, with great success, to stimulating world farm output. The task at hand in 1985 is not to encourage farm output in all countries in all crops, but to begin rationalizing production on a global basis.

Textiles and Apparel

Tariffs on trade in textiles and apparel have stayed high throughout the postwar period. In addition, textile and apparel trade has been subject to an increasing array of quantitative restraints since the 1957 US-Japan voluntary restraint agreement on cotton textiles.[26] Protection has been virtually institutionalized, governed successively by a Short-Term and a Long-Term Arrangement on Cotton Textiles, and three iterations of the Multi-Fiber Arrangement (MFA). The number of participating countries and the range of products subject to controls continue to grow. Today, MFA III serves as the framework for bilateral restraint agreements among 17 developed countries and 34 developing countries, covering trade in cotton, wool, many man-made fibers, and apparel items. Only a handful of countries (for example, Australia, New Zealand, Norway) restrict textile and apparel trade through GATT Article XIX safeguards rather than under the MFA.

With few exceptions, tariffs are the most important barrier to trade *between*

---

25. Hufbauer and Rosen, *Trade Policy for Troubled Industries*, ch. 7.

26. This agreement revived the restraints placed on Japanese cotton textile exports during the interwar period by the United States and by most European countries.

developed countries. In fact, the industrial countries generally exempt one another from the apparatus of QRs. Average tariffs for textiles and apparel in the OECD area, however, remain high (19.0 percent in the United States; 11.5 percent in Europe; 11.5 percent in Japan). In the Tokyo Round, textile and apparel tariffs were reduced on average by only 17.5 percent of their pre-Round level, compared to an average reduction of 34 percent for all products.[27]

By contrast, most trade *between developed and developing countries* is effectively restrained by bilateral quotas negotiated under the MFA. To be sure, textile imports from LDC suppliers also pay high tariffs when they enter individual OECD countries, but quantitative restrictions usually furnish the binding constraint. Similarly, many developing countries maintain restrictions of their own on textile and apparel imports to protect local industries and to preserve foreign exchange.

TRADE EXPANSION DESPITE PROTECTION

Despite these formidable controls, textile and apparel trade has grown markedly. Between 1963 and 1983, the value of world exports of textiles and apparel grew at an average annual rate of 12.4 percent, slightly trailing the 13.6 percent growth rate for all manufactured exports. Textile and apparel trade now totals almost $100 billion a year, constituting about 9 percent of all manufactured exports.[28]

Germany, Japan, and Italy are the leading exporters of *textiles*. China is the only developing country among the top 10 exporters, but is gaining fast on the leaders with an annual export growth rate of more than 15 percent for the past decade. By contrast, most of the major exporters of *apparel* are developing countries. Hong Kong, Italy, and Korea are the leading exporters, although the growth of Chinese exports of apparel from 1973 to 1982 far outpaced that of any of the other leading exporters, growing at an annual rate of 30.5 percent.[29]

Industrial countries account for a large portion of imports of textiles and

27. GATT, *Textiles and Clothing in the World Economy*, vol. 1, (Geneva, July 1984), p. 68.

28. GATT, *Textiles and Clothing*, pp. 40–41.

29. GATT, *Textiles and Clothing*, pp. 42–43.

apparel. In 1983, their share of world textile imports was approximately 54 percent; their share of apparel imports was nearly 80 percent. Germany, the United Kingdom, the United States, and France were the major textile importers; the United States, with imports of $10.4 billion, was the leading apparel importer.[30] Promoted by recovery and a high dollar, US imports of textiles and apparel have increased further, up about 41 percent in volume in 1984 over 1983.[31]

As in the Prohibition era, protection has spawned new suppliers and substitute products. Man-made fibers, such as acrylics, now replace textiles whose trade is restrained by MFA quotas, while production has moved to countries, such as Fiji, not covered by bilateral restraints negotiated under the MFA rubric. Producers in OECD countries clamor for more protection through comprehensive global quotas overlaid on more restrictive bilateral quotas, while traditional LDC exporters hotly pursue easier access to OECD markets.

In the OECD area, the major problem is employment: because new, labor-saving investments have increased productivity, labor will continue to be displaced, even if the import share of the market remains constant. Indeed, to stabilize employment in the OECD area, the MFA-sanctioned quotas against the LDCs would have to provide a very substantial *rollback* in the volume of imports.

For LDCs, the problems are diverse. All want the volume of OECD imports to rise. This is particularly important for debt-ridden LDCs that need export growth in textiles, apparel, and other manufactured goods. Certain less competitive LDCs want the system of bilateral quotas to continue, thereby guaranteeing their market access in the face of strong competition from China and other LDCs; others want the MFA regime to lapse, thereby giving them free reign to exploit their comparative advantage.

RENEW, THEN RETIRE, MFA III

MFA III comes up for renewal in July 1986. Negotiations on whether to extend the MFA, and if so in what shape and form, have already begun.

---

30. GATT, *International Trade 1983/84*, p. A11.

31. See table 3.1. There are three important sources of recent US import growth: noncovered fibers, such as handloom goods; imports from Europe, spurred by the strong dollar; and imports from LDC suppliers that had not filled their quotas or were not covered by bilateral quotas.

While clear lines have not yet been drawn, the basic options are: (1) to renew the MFA, but to allow an even tighter set of restrictions in bilateral agreements; (2) to abandon the MFA and return to GATT safeguard principles for the textile and apparel industry; and (3) to renew the MFA, but provide for the progressive relaxation of quotas.

From the standpoint of the OECD countries, the first option represents the path of least political resistance. In the United States, for example, the industry has pushed the Textile and Apparel Trade Enforcement Act of 1985 (H.R. 1562), a bill that would first roll back US imports and then virtually eliminate future growth. This legislation is enormously popular in Congress, and by May 1985 had acquired 275 cosponsors in the House and 40 in the Senate.[32] On the other hand, many LDCs will find little interest in new trade talks if there is no OECD commitment to liberalize textile and apparel trade. Moreover, if textile and apparel restraints are permanently tightened, many industrial countries will encounter greater difficulty mustering the political coalitions required to liberalize trade in steel, automobiles, agriculture, and other troubled industries.

The complete elimination of the MFA regime is equally impractical. Some economists might extol the virtues of an immediate return to free trade, but almost every producer (except perhaps China and Hong Kong) would object; given the distortions in production and trade patterns built up over decades of protection, immediate liberalization would result in major dislocation.

We conclude that the MFA system needs to be phased out, but very slowly. A phased retirement would encourage adjustment, yet provide time for an orderly transition and temporarily safeguard the market access of minor LDC suppliers in OECD markets. The system of bilateral quotas under the MFA should be continued for several years, but negotiations should establish a schedule of liberalization that returns textile and apparel trade to GATT discipline by the year 2000.

Such an agreement is improbable before the expiration of the MFA in July 1986. Thus, for reasons of timing, the MFA should be rolled over in its present shape, and renewal and retirement talks should take place in the Growth Round. If developed and developing countries alike are going to retire the MFA by the year 2000, three concerns will have to be met over the next fifteen years:

---

32. *Journal of Commerce*, 24 May 1985, p. 1A. By July 1985, the number of Senate cosponsors reached 53 and House cosponsors, 283.

- Producers in OECD countries will need assurance that they will not be swamped by imports from new and old suppliers, and that they will obtain liberal assistance in adjustment programs that help downsize the industry.

- Many LDCs will need assurance that *their* exporters will not be suddenly knocked out of foreign markets by goods from China, Hong Kong, and India. Their industries need time to downsize as well.

- OECD governments need assurance that intra-OECD trade, currently not subject to quotas, will not be severely disrupted by a phase-out of restrictions on LDC exports.

These three points address important *political* concerns. Almost thirty years of trade restraints have created sheltered industries and workers who will not accept significant change unless their interests are accommodated.

Our solution combines three strategies: self-financed adjustment, an umbrella of temporary protection, and gradual growth in the volume of trade subject to market forces. As a starting point, each major importing nation would establish a system of global quotas on major individual textile and apparel categories covering suppliers from all countries. At the outset, the global level would be based on the volume of imports in the final year of MFA III. Individual country quotas would be maintained within the global quota. In the case of exporting countries not previously subject to bilateral restraints, the quota levels would be set with reference to recent trade levels.

Each year the global quota for each importing country would be expanded by 6 percent; at the same time, the national quota of each exporting country would be reduced by 10 percent. The unallocated quota rights (i.e., the 6 percent increase in the aggregate level, plus 10 percent of the existing national quotas) would then be auctioned off by the importing country to the highest bidder. Over a period of time, national quotas would be reduced to zero, while the global quotas would be expanded to the point that they no longer restricted trade flows. In other words, the supply of quota rights would reach a level where the price of the rights approached zero.

Table 3.1 illustrates how this system would work, with rough calculations of the effect of this scheme for the United States. The global US import quota, based on 1984 levels, would be almost 3.0 billion pounds, representing 20.4 percent of US consumption. Over the next decade, the global quota would increase by 6 percent a year to almost 5.4 billion pounds, accounting

T A B L E   3.1   **Hypothetical US textile and apparel trade under a revised MFA (million pounds and percentage)**

	US exports	US imports	Fixed national quotas	US production	US consumption	Imports/ consumption
Actual						
1980	1,319	1,455	n.a.	11,890	12,026	12.1
1981	1,017	1,715	n.a.	11,548	12,246	14.0
1982	704	1,707	n.a.	10,100	11,103	15.4
1983	701	2,160	n.a.	12,096	13,555	15.9
1984	684	2,992	2,992	12,328	14,636	20.4
Projected[a]						
1985	735	3,172	2,693	12,492	14,929	21.2
1986	790	3,362	2,424	12,655	15,227	22.1
1987	850	3,564	2,181	12,818	15,532	22.9
1988	913	3,777	1,963	12,978	15,842	23.8
1989	982	4,004	1,767	13,137	16,159	24.8
1990	1,056	4,244	1,590	13,295	16,483	25.7
1991	1,135	4,499	1,431	13,448	16,812	26.7
1992	1,220	4,769	1,288	13,599	17,148	27.8
1993	1,311	5,055	1,159	13,747	17,491	28.9
1994	1,410	5,358	1,043	13,893	17,841	30.0

n.a. Not applicable.

Source: US Commerce Department, International Trade Administration, *Major Shippers of Cotton, Wool, and Man-made Fiber Textiles and Apparel,* various issues; US International Trade Commission, *US Imports of Textiles and Apparel under the Multi-Fiber Arrangement 1976–1983,* USITC pub. no. 1539, June 1984; and *US Imports of Textiles and Apparel under the Multi-Fiber Arrangement, January–June 1984,* USITC pub. no. 1635, January 1985.

a. The projections assume 2 percent annual growth in US consumption; 100 percent utilization of global import quotas, which increase by 6 percent a year; and 7.5 percent annual growth in US exports (thereby maintaining the average ratio of exports to US production over the period 1974–83). Projected US production is calculated as a residual derived by adding consumption and exports and subtracting imports. Once the foreign exchange value of the dollar reaches more competitive levels, exports could do better than the projections in the table.

for some 30 percent of US consumption in 1994 (a 50 percent increase in the import-consumption ratio).[33] At the same time, however, US production would increase because of a resurgence in US exports fostered by liberalization of import restrictions in overseas markets. Once the dollar returns to more

---

33. To the extent domestic producers can meet world competition, there will be less demand for the quota rights, less import competition, and thus less need to adjust.

competitive levels, the US textile industry should gain new markets overseas even as the US apparel industry faces stronger import competition.

Over time, national quotas would decline by 10 percent a year from 3.0 billion pounds to around 1.0 billion pounds in 1994. As a result, quota rights for 4.4 billion pounds of imports (the global quota of 5.4 billion less the fixed national quotas of 1.0 billion) would be auctioned off by the US government to the highest bidders, presumably the most competitive suppliers.

The proceeds from the quota auctions, together with existing tariff revenues, should be dedicated to adjustment programs for the domestic textile and apparel industry. Calculations made elsewhere indicate that the tariff and quota revenues would prove adequate to fund very liberal worker retraining, retirement, and redeployment programs.[34] These calculations indicate that, over the period 1985 to 1990, the adjustment program could finance the exit of about 2.4 percent of the labor force annually (about 47,000 workers) of which some 40 percent would depart in any event due to productivity growth. The average costs of retraining workers (coupled with necessary income maintenance), early retirement in appropriate cases, and absorbing the tax-loss carry-forwards generated by plant shutdowns, are liberally estimated at $35,000 per departing worker. This is nearly 10 times the costs per worker incurred under the Trade Adjustment Assistance program. Even so, under the partial system of auctioned quotas proposed here (assigned national quotas declining year by year), the revenues would approximately equal the program costs (about $10 billion spread over six years).

The system of quota auctions would encourage exports from the most efficient suppliers. Inefficient LDC *exporters*, currently protected by MFA quotas, would have to adjust as their assigned quota rights were retired. Indeed, noncompetitive suppliers that want to accelerate the adjustment process should be free to sell their assigned quota rights to other countries and to use the proceeds to enter new industries.[35]

Meanwhile, global quotas would protect OECD producers from the huge and unpredictable import volume increases that they now face. In return for the predictability of global quotas and very much larger and more creative

---

34. Gary Clyde Hufbauer, Diane T. Berliner, and Kimberly Ann Elliott, *Trade Protection in the United States: 31 Case Studies* (Washington: Institute for International Economics, forthcoming 1985).

35. An internal quota auction market among local suppliers already exists in Hong Kong.

adjustment programs, OECD producers should consent to open their markets gradually to import competition.

High Technology Trade

While there is no standard definition of high technology products, the OECD has compiled a list that includes computers, electronic and telecommunications equipment, pharmaceuticals, scientific instruments, and certain electrical and nonelectrical machinery. The list is constantly evolving, however, as various industries incorporate the latest technological innovations.

Most high technology products are capital intensive and require large research and development (R&D) expenditures. This capital can be generated from a large volume of sales at home and abroad, from subsidies from home governments, and from reserved government procurement markets.

Trade in high technology products accounted for an estimated 17.5 percent of total OECD manufactured exports in 1983; among these products, computers and electronic equipment contributed the fastest export growth since 1970. The United States, the United Kingdom, and Switzerland each account for more than 20 percent of OECD exports of high technology products; Japan, Germany, and France account for most of the rest. The United States has also been the largest importer of high technology products, accounting for about 23 percent of OECD imports. Almost half of US imports come from Japan; Canada supplies almost 20 percent; Germany, the United Kingdom, and France provide most of the rest.[36] US officials cite the ''openness'' of US markets compared to other countries as an important reason why the US trade surplus in high technology products fell from $26 billion in 1980 to $6.2 billion in 1984.[37] Industry sources, however, place more emphasis on the strong dollar.

The United States is particularly concerned about access to foreign markets in computers and telecommunications equipment, and financial and information services. Purchases by many public telecommunications monopolies are excluded from the discipline of the GATT government procurement code and are effectively restricted to domestic suppliers.

---

36. Data are from the OECD Directorate of Science, Technology, and Industry.

37. Timothy J. Hauser, ''The Case for Addressing High Technology Trade in the New Trade Round'' (Remarks to the Patronat, Paris, 21 March 1985), p. 5.

Other countries are equally concerned about access to US-based research and US high technology products, and sales to the large US government procurement market. This problem has become particularly vexing in light of the massive R&D expenditures that are projected for the US Strategic Defense Initiative, or "Star Wars" program. Moreover, Europeans remember well their experience with US sanctions against the European-Soviet gas pipeline, and they seek assurances concerning the future flow of technology and the exercise of US extraterritorial claims on foreign subsidiaries. This subject also concerns the LDCs. Argentina, for example, complained about US export controls during the 1982 Falklands war and questioned the stated US justification, namely the national security exception of GATT Article XXI.

Developing countries also are concerned about the increasing cost of participating in the technological race. Large capital requirements are driving many of their high technology firms below the R&D "poverty line." In developed countries this problem is often resolved through corporate takeovers, creating firms large enough to fund R&D requirements and to exploit new commercial opportunities on a global scale. Few LDCs have the firms or the resources to follow this path. Instead, they must rely on transfers of technology through the purchase of "turnkey" plants and equipment, along with the provision of technical services. Many LDCs require compulsory licensing of patents, or simply do not grant patents in important branches of production (such as chemicals and software), as a way of breaking what they perceive as the technological monopoly of industrial countries. Brazil has taken an alternative tack, attempting to develop an indigenous informatics sector through buy-national government procurement and extreme trade protection from foreign competition.

Tariffs remain a significant trade barrier in the high technology sector, although the tariff profile differs significantly across products and countries. Tariffs are particularly high in the telecommunications sector, especially for those products with high R&D costs.

The primary objectives for new trade talks in the high technology area should be market access (including discipline on R&D subsidies, the ability to compete for government contracts, and tariff reductions), the free flow of data across borders, and protection of intellectual property rights. These objectives do *not* require a separate sectoral negotiation on high technology products. The importance of this sector, however, argues that priority attention be given to measures that distort high technology trade. High technology thus appears as a recurring theme in the negotiating strategies for subsidies, services, intellectual property, and tariffs.

Subsidies

Despite the GATT Code on Subsidies and Countervailing Measures developed during the Tokyo Round, subsidies remain a pervasive form of import protection and export promotion.[38] Subsidies lie at the heart of the "fairness" question. They are a growing ingredient of disputes over high technology trade.

Problems with subsidized trade have drawn attention to the limitations of GATT discipline. Export subsidies, those which favor exported products over goods sold on the home market, are generally prohibited by the Subsidies Code, but agricultural goods are virtually exempt from this ban. Not surprisingly, most GATT disputes have centered on export subsidies that promote agricultural sales. In addition, code provisions are not very constraining with regard to domestic subsidies, namely subsidies that make no distinction between goods sold abroad and goods sold at home.

The fact that the Subsidies Code has not worked well is scarcely an argument for abandoning international discipline; rather it provides a compelling reason to seek better solutions through new negotiations. Three priority problems need to be addressed: improved rules on agricultural export subsidies and official export credits, new provisions that spell out the permitted range of domestic subsidies, and new remedies to answer subsidized export competition in third-country markets.[39]

EXPORT SUBSIDIES

Almost all countries subsidize the farm sector and some countries heavily subsidize the export of agricultural goods. This hurts countries that depend

---

38. Nevertheless, the attention given to subsidies in trade policy discussions probably far surpasses the amount of trade affected. In the period 1982–84, the value of US imports subject to either countervailing or antidumping duties was about $2.9 billion, about 1 percent of total US imports. See *Journal of Commerce*, 21 May 1985, p. 17A.

39. These are not the only subsidy issues that deserve attention. A more comprehensive examination of subsidy problems, with recommendations for their resolution, appears in Gary Clyde Hufbauer and Joanna Shelton Erb, *Subsidies in International Trade* (Washington: Institute for International Economics, 1984).

on agricultural exports: Australia, Argentina, Canada, New Zealand, and the United States. In the context of an overall solution to the agricultural production problems discussed above, agricultural export subsidies should eventually be brought under the same discipline as other export subsidies. It may take several years to reach this goal; subsidies would have to be phased out slowly. A first step would involve a degressive cap on the volume of agricultural output receiving export subsidies.

Apart from agriculture, the main area of export subsidy competition is official export credits. The International Arrangement on Official Export Credits (the "Gentlemen's Agreement" or "Consensus") provides discipline over the interest rates, terms, and maturities of official export credits. The arrangement is subject to abuse, however, in the area of mixed credits (official export credits mixed with grant aid). Illustrative of mixed-credit practices was the competition for construction of a bridge over the Bosporus in Turkey, pitting British and Japanese aid and export credit agencies in a contest of offering the Turks the most aid and the cheapest credit.[40] The solution to mixed-credit competition is a requirement that the grant element must be very high, say 40 percent or more, or the credit will be subject to the normal rules of the Consensus. A rule of this sort would ensure that aid is really aid, not export credits masquerading as aid.

DOMESTIC SUBSIDIES

Domestic subsidies, those that make no distinction between goods sold at home and goods sold abroad, lie at the heart of national attempts to interfere in the economy for constructive purposes. At the same time, they provoke loud complaints that the playing field is tilted. A semiconductor manufacturer in Silicon Valley asks how he can compete with a manufacturer in Osaka if the Japanese firm has a guaranteed domestic market and government R&D support as well. Such practices are not condemned outright by the Subsidies Code. Instead, importing countries may impose offsetting countermeasures, but only when the subsidized imports cause the requisite degree of injury to local industry.

---

40. *Wall Street Journal*, 29 May 1985, p. 1. The winning Japanese bid of $561 million provided $205 million in government loans, at 5 percent interest, repayable over 25 years with a seven-year grace period. Under the consensus, the most generous terms would have been 11.20 percent over 10 years.

The difficulty with this approach is that there is considerable uncertainty as to which domestic incentive practices would be potentially subject to countervailing duties if they lead to injurious trade. To date, efforts to define a "positive" list of domestic subsidies have been unrewarding. Two troublesome areas are off-budget incentives (for example, preferential access to valuable minerals) and incentives that are "generally available" to a large class of individuals or firms (for example, subsidized credit for business expansion). Signatories to the Subsidies Code have not been able to agree on which off-budget incentives and which "generally available" subsidies should be countervailed. The impasse might be bridged from a different angle: agreement might be reached that certain types of incentives are permissible and will *not* be subject to countervailing measures.

For example, a sharp distinction should be made between government-sponsored research that is made publicly available and government-sponsored research that is retained on a proprietary basis. If computer research funded by the Japanese government were made available on a timely basis to all firms—American and German, as well as Japanese—then new products based on this research should not be subject to countervailing duties. On the other hand, if computer research funded by the Japanese government is made available on a preferential basis to Japanese firms, then products shipped by those firms should be liable to countervailing duties. Research for military purposes clearly must be restricted; however, when firms develop commercial applications from military research, the products should be exempt from countervailing duties only if they emerge more than, say, five years after the R&D subsidies were granted.

Allowance should be made for domestic subsidies that are used to further adjustment. The British government put a tremendous amount of money into British Steel to close inefficient plants and reduce the labor force by half. Sweden did the same in its textile industry. Such assistance is clearly a subsidy, but it is a "good" subsidy. The Subsidies Code, however, makes no exception for funds used to downsize troubled industries. A change is needed. The rules should *encourage* subsidies that are dedicated to effective adjustment programs.

The bargain sale of natural resource rights represents an important form of off-budget incentive that might or might not be regarded as a troublesome domestic subsidy. This is a thorny issue. Many countries view the disposition of natural resource rights as a sovereign action that may properly be used to further economic goals (recall the US Homestead Acts), but competing producers abroad often regard such actions as unfair competition.

To reconcile these competing views, countries should agree that the bargain sale of the right to exploit *nontransportable* resources would not be considered as a countervailable domestic incentive. After all, most firms that are lucky enough to acquire scarce resource rights at bargain terms will not toss away their good fortune by selling output at below-market prices. If the sale is *conditioned* on export obligations, by law or by the nature of the product (for example, there is very little home consumption, and holders of resource rights are required to develop at a certain rate), then the incentive should be liable for countervailing duties. In these circumstances, the export obligation will prod firms to sell output at below-market prices. In addition, any domestic incentive system that sells *transportable* natural resources such as oil or logs to domestic producers at prices below world market levels should be regarded as conveying a countervailable domestic subsidy. The bargain sale of oil to a refinery, for example, more closely resembles a cash subsidy than the sovereign disposition of land rights.

It may well turn out that international rules defining these and other domestic subsidies will not emerge from the process of negotiation. Instead, it may require the increased use of countervailing duties by various countries—the European Community, Canada, Japan, and Brazil, as well as the United States—to define permissible and impermissible domestic subsidies on a case-by-case basis. As countervailing duties are used more widely, countries will come to see the problems both as importers and as exporters. For example, Boeing and IBM might develop a lively interest in persuading the US Commerce Department to limit its definition of countervailable R&D subsidies, if those firms faced countervailing duty actions in the European market. Pressure then might build to harmonize differences in national approaches through negotiations.

THIRD-COUNTRY MARKETS

A major weakness of present GATT discipline on subsidies is that the rules offer little assistance to a country that loses third-country export markets to the subsidized trade of a competitor. For example, US exports of PL 480 wheat to Indonesia may damage Australian export prospects, but Australia gets little or no relief by closing its home market to US wheat or by calling for a GATT panel. Two new remedies could be put in place to answer these third-country market problems.

First, with prior approval by the Subsidies Code Committee, the injured country should be permitted to levy a low-rate tariff on *all* its imports from the subsidizing country, and then dedicate the proceeds to matching the subsidy competition in the third-country market. Second, code signatories should permit one another access to their domestic proceedings to impose countervailing duties against an offending third country.

Countertrade requirements may mask subsidies which, like the US PL 480 program or the EC CAP, harm the export opportunities of countries that are not party to the transaction. Unlike many subsidy practices, however, countertrade transactions lack transparency. To pierce the secrecy barrier, countries should notify all countertrade transactions valued over, say, $10 million to the GATT. Injured third countries could then invoke the new remedies as appropriate.

Services

The service sector represents a large part of the modern economy and an important source of job creation. For example, nongovernment services contributed more than 70 percent of the 20 million new jobs created in the US economy in the 1970s. By contrast, manufacturing employment grew by only 1 million jobs. Nongovernment service activities account for more than 50 percent of US GNP. The services share of GNP of other major industrial countries also is in the 40 percent to 50 percent range.

Services trade grew on average by almost 20 percent per year during the 1970s, in lockstep with the growth in merchandise trade. By conservative estimates, global services trade in 1980 totaled about $500 billion, or approximately 20 percent of global trade in goods and services.[41] The growth of international trade in services reflects the cumulative effect of two important developments. First, the liberalization of goods markets and key capital markets opened up new international opportunities for services industries. Second, and perhaps more important, advances in telecommunications facilitated the rapid transmission of data over large distances, enabling services industries to operate on an international scale.

One can argue that international trade in services has progressed rather

---

41. Available statistics likely underestimate the value of trade in services. The figures cited here are from IMF sources and data compiled by the Committee on Invisible Exports, London.

well without a general set of rules parallel to those set forth in the GATT for trade in goods.[42] Where needed, international agreements have been developed for sectors such as civil aviation and shipping. Perhaps GATT should leave well enough alone and stay clear of services trade.

There are broader reasons, however, why GATT rules on services are important. Services transactions are increasingly "commingled" with the production and trade of goods. Companies today rely on advanced communications systems to coordinate planning, production, and distribution of products. Computer software helps to design new products and to run the robots that produce them. Some firms engage in-house lawyers, accountants, and engineers; some have "captive" subsidiaries to handle their insurance and finance needs. In other words, services are both inputs for the production of manufactured goods (from engineering design to data processing) and necessary complements in organizing trade (from financing and insuring the transaction to providing after-sales maintenance, especially critical for large capital goods). Thus, it is no longer possible to talk about freer trade in goods without talking about freer trade in services.

The United States has compiled an impressive list of restrictions that interfere with international transactions of service companies. Some of the restrictions take the same form as those applied to goods, tariffs, import licenses, quotas, subsidies, and discriminatory government procurement policies. Other restrictions hamper trade in services by limiting investment opportunities, or by restricting access to data banks, information systems and communications networks.

GATT negotiations need to tackle three complementary tasks. First, negotiations should seek a standstill agreement on new services trade barriers. Second, negotiators should develop a general framework of rules in the shape of an "umbrella" code. As part of that process, several of the existing Tokyo Round codes should be adapted to cover services transactions. Third, governments need to address specific services trade problems, including those that stem from regulatory policies and from controls on transborder data flows.

---

42. The question of rules for trade in services is not new. The Havana Charter for an International Trade Organization included an article on services trade in the final text negotiated by the United States and 56 other countries in March 1948 (but never ratified). For a survey of current barriers to trade in services, see Jeffrey J. Schott, "Protectionist Threat to Trade and Investment in Services," *The World Economy*, vol. 6, no. 2 (June 1983).

STANDSTILL ON SERVICES RESTRICTIONS

Unlike the standstill on merchandise trade, which should be implemented at the start of the Growth Round by all countries and without compensation, a standstill on services trade barriers represents an important negotiating objective in itself. A standstill would have several purposes: to make barriers explicit; to ensure an arm's length relationship between government regulation (for example, of the insurance industry) and the operation of publicly owned companies; and to prevent a proliferation of new barriers. The last goal is particularly important. For example, foreign access to the US banking sector and telecommunications market is today relatively unfettered, but failure to achieve reciprocal export opportunities may result in a wave of new restrictions.

A standstill agreement would require consensus on which restrictions serve legitimate purposes (for example, public health standards and prudential standards for financial institutions) and which unduly distort trade. Negotiations on a standstill would thus proceed alongside the development of more general GATT rules on services.

"UMBRELLA" CODE

The Tokyo Round codes represent understandings between signatories on how they will interpret and implement *existing* GATT articles. Since there is no general body of rules on services in the GATT, and since it is unlikely that all 93 GATT members will consent to amend the existing GATT articles, a Services Code would stand apart from the basic GATT framework. It could be linked, however, to basic GATT notification, consultation, and enforcement provisions, and it should be open to all GATT members on a conditional MFN basis.

A Services Code should focus on three broad principles that would serve as guideposts for national policies. First is transparency: services trade barriers need to be notified and exposed to consultation and dispute settlement procedures. Second is nondiscrimination as between domestic and foreign firms, or the extension of the national treatment principle to the services sector. Third is the right to transact business: foreign firms should be free to establish ventures on the same footing as local firms. At a minimum, OECD governments should commit themselves to these three principles, with exceptions for narrowly defined national security, health and safety, and prudential concerns.

Some specificity must be given to the scope of these principles. Certain areas would cause difficulty. In the civil aviation and maritime sectors, the right of establishment would translate into an "open skies" regime and permission for all vessels to ply the coastal trades. In contract construction, right of establishment would allow, for example, Korean construction firms to operate in the United States. In health care, it would allow Hospital Corporation of America to open facilities in London, Paris, or Tokyo. In some cases, rendering the service is closely linked to immigration (contract construction and coastal maritime services); in other cases, right of establishment would intrude on government monopolies (civil aviation and health care). To deal with these problems, governments could negotiate, in the first instance, which sectors would be subject to code obligations, with a commitment to expand coverage after a review period.[43]

Beyond broad principles, specific concessions will be needed to demonstrate that new opportunities are opened as a result of trade talks. Liberalization will require implicit trade-offs between sectors and within sectors, a process that is never easy. The manufacturing sector in the United States, for example, does not want to be a chip in a larger effort to pry open foreign banking markets, or value-added networks. Similarly, shipping does not want to be traded for insurance. Life insurance does not want to make concessions for casualty insurance. No country will agree to dismantle its own politically sensitive barriers without compensation, however. Trade-offs must be made. There can be no hermetic seal between services negotiations and goods negotiations if the objective is to reduce trade barriers.[44]

Many services trade problems can be addressed directly in a GATT context. There is ample scope to extend the Tokyo Round codes to deal with practices that distort services trade, in particular, subsidies, licensing controls, technical standards, and restrictive government procurement policies. Both the Government Procurement Code and the Subsidies Code already cover certain

---

43. Such an approach would follow the precedent of the Government Procurement Code, where negotiations on a covered list of entities determined which transactions would come under the code rules.

44. In June 1985, Brazil proposed separate negotiations on trade in goods (in GATT) and trade in services (outside GATT), without trade-offs of concessions between the two talks. Such a scheme is impractical and undesirable: implicit economic and political linkages exist on all issues in any event, and an attempted separation might delay major trade reforms. In particular, such an approach would sidetrack efforts to liberalize products of interest to Brazil such as steel, textiles, and apparel.

services transactions. The former covers the procurement of "services incidental to the supply of products"; the latter prohibits, for example, certain transport and freight subsidies that benefit industrial exports. In addition, the Government Procurement Code commits signatories to "explore the possibilities of expanding the coverage to include service contracts" during the review of code provisions which is currently underway in Geneva. This would be particularly important for major public construction and engineering projects, and for telecommunications and data processing services purchased by public corporations.

REGULATORY BARRIERS

Concerns about regulatory barriers to trade in services focus on discrimination against foreign firms applied by various levels of government. The United States, Canada, and Germany, for example, can expect demands that state and provincial regulators not be allowed to undercut free trade commitments entered into by federal negotiators. More than a "best-efforts" commitment is needed to allay foreign concerns about the real value of undertakings at the federal level: similar pledges in the context of the Government Procurement Code have not cured the protectionist instincts of various state and provincial legislatures.

The priority concerns of foreign governments in dealing with the United States can be addressed if the federal government conducts a parallel negotiation with the key states involved, notably New York, California, and Illinois. In return for a commitment by a state to follow a certain regulatory policy (thereby mitigating a foreign trade complaint), the federal government could offer a suitable concession.[45] The negotiation would be conducted between federal and state authorities, similar to talks held every day on dozens of different issues. A similar approach may be useful in Canada, Germany, and other countries with strong subfederal governments.

---

45. Plausible concessions would entail measures to resolve specific foreign trade problems of priority concern to industries in the individual state during the trade negotiations; they would not involve other functional areas, such as revenue-sharing formulas for dividing funds between state and local governments.

TRANSBORDER DATA FLOWS

Restrictions on telecommunications services, and the cross-border flow of data in particular, may be fertile ground for a new wave of controls. US controls on the data transmissions of Dresser Industries to its overseas subsidiaries during the Soviet gas pipeline sanctions in 1982 demonstrated the potential danger. In that instance, the US government barred the transmission of technical data to Dresser's French subsidiary, effectively blocking current production of compressors in France (the purpose of the sanctions) and placing Dresser-France at a competitive disadvantage in bidding on other, non-controversial orders.

OECD countries addressed this issue in a declaration on transborder data flows, adopted at the April 1985 Ministerial, which commits member countries to "avoid the creation of unjustified barriers to the international exchange of data and information."[46] Since the OECD declaration does not commit countries to alter existing national policies, the potential for mischief still remains.

To supplement the OECD effort, negotiations should be undertaken on a priority basis and in parallel to the GATT talks to develop a standstill agreement on all taxes and border restrictions that inhibit data flows. Because it may take years to negotiate an accord on data flows in the OECD or the GATT, it would be better to try to work out a pact among key countries (for example, the United States, the European Community, Sweden, Switzerland, Canada, Japan) at a separate conference convened exclusively for that purpose. Once an accord is reached, the signatories should try to obtain a consensus among a broader group of countries in the new GATT round, and turn their thoughts to eliminating existing barriers.

Investment

Investment issues are not dealt with in the GATT, yet many government policies on foreign direct investment also influence trade flows. Export performance requirements linked to investment incentives both distort investment decisions as to the location of plants and effectively subsidize future

---

46. OECD, *Declaration on Transborder Data Flows*, Paris, 11 April 1985.

production from those plants. Moreover, such incentives and requirements often affect a company's decision to invest in a foreign subsidiary rather than to export to that country. Restrictions on the right of establishment limit the types of activity and increase the costs to foreign firms doing business abroad, particularly in the services sector.

Because investment has always been a politically sensitive issue, scant progress has been made toward developing international rules on foreign direct investment that would discipline national policies of both host and donor countries. Ten years of talks in the United Nations context have failed to produce a code of conduct for multinational corporations; the outlook for progress in the GATT on a code of conduct for government behavior seems equally remote. In the course of a comprehensive trade negotiation, however, there may be an opportunity to reach key objectives through a broad-based exchange of concessions.

The combined effects of the global recession and the LDC debt crisis have led to a broad reassessment of national policies by countries that traditionally have opposed international rules. Canada, for one, has become much more receptive to foreign investment; India also is encouraging new investment from abroad in the high technology and other sectors. In addition, some debt-ridden LDCs are seeking more foreign direct investment as a substitute for increased commercial bank lending.[47]

Negotiations could build on the progress achieved in the OECD codes on invisibles and on capital movements, and in the various bilateral investment agreements initiated by the United States, the United Kingdom, Switzerland, and Germany. These agreements were basically set up to espouse general principles of international law, but they can certainly be adapted to new problems in the international investment field.

Following these precedents, countries should design a framework of broad rules and principles before addressing specific problems. An agreement should focus on three main issues: nondiscrimination, the right of establishment, and investment incentives coupled with performance requirements.

First, countries should agree to treat foreign-owned firms, in all forms of regulation and government programs, as they treat domestic firms. Limited exceptions could be provided for sensitive sectors such as defense and public communications. Such a pledge would be more comprehensive than the

---

47. For a more detailed discussion, see William E. Brock, "Trade and Debt: The Vital Linkage," *Foreign Affairs,* vol. 62, no. 5 (Summer 1984).

OECD declaration on national treatment, which allows a wide range of exceptions.

Second, countries should provide for free establishment for all manufacturing and service firms, subject to limited exceptions for national security reasons and designated sensitive sectors. Free establishment rights would be phased in over time. For some sectors (such as financial services), it may also be possible to reach agreement on common minimum criteria for national regulations on the establishment of banks and insurance companies.

Third, while investment incentives, like domestic subsidies, are not objectionable per se, they cause substantial trade friction when combined with performance requirements. Countries should agree not to provide investment incentives contingent on trade-distorting performance requirements (for example, local content rules and minimum export requirements).

In addition, the GATT should establish a consultative body, perhaps akin to the ''cathedral'' that was proposed for agricultural issues at the end of the Tokyo Round. Such a forum would have two purposes: (1) to discuss trade-related investment issues at the macro level (such as the role of foreign direct investment in helping to resolve LDC trade and debt problems), and (2) to review specific investment issues that may arise in negotiations (such as performance requirements, investment incentives, and establishment rules for services sectors).

Intellectual Property

Intellectual property rights are protected internationally under the provisions of several conventions: (1) the Paris Convention of 1883 for the Protection of Intellectual Property, which sets minimum standards for national legislation and provides some nondiscrimination guarantees; (2) the Universal Copyright Convention of 1952; (3) the Patent Cooperation Treaty of 1970; and (4) the charter of the World Intellectual Property Organization (WIPO), established in December 1974 as part of the United Nations system.

Despite this overlapping network of international regulation, the arcane and complex issues of intellectual property have recently caught the attention of trade policy officials. It is now widely recognized that national laws and administrative procedures in the intellectual property area can create effective nontariff barriers to trade and disincentives to innovation and technology transfer. It is further recognized that the existing conventions and agreements are virtually devoid of effective enforcement mechanisms.

The problems are particularly acute in high technology areas such as design patents for software, semiconductor chips, and biotechnology advances. Many high technology firms in the United States and Europe see their basic capital "pirated" by competitors in Korea, India, Taiwan, and other countries. US trade officials regard this issue as one of their top priorities and have pressed other countries, under the threat of exclusion from the US market if reciprocal protection is not granted, to modify their national patent, copyright, and trademark laws.

PATENTS, COPYRIGHTS, AND TRADEMARKS

Patents, copyrights, and trademarks are the core of intellectual property. Patent rights provide monopoly protection to the holder for a limited time period covering the manufacture and distribution of a product or a process. Monopoly rights are intended to provide incentives both for innovative activity and for the disclosure of inventions. Copyrights protect the right to reproduce, to publish, and to sell written works, art, and music. Trademark rights are designed to safeguard the holder's use of a proprietary name.

The list of international problems in the implementation of national patent, copyright, and trademark laws is long. The scope of patent protection differs greatly from country to country, both as to kinds of inventions eligible for patent protection and as to requirements for obtaining a patent. Certain products (such as chemical compounds) are simply not eligible for patent protection in some countries. In addition, administrative delays can be used to "steal" the property rights, to prompt their license at reduced prices, or to reduce the effective period of protection. Compulsory licensing requirements often force patent holders to manufacture locally instead of importing in order to maintain the exclusive right to the patent.

The conditions of copyright and trademark protection are often used as trade barriers. For example, countries such as Mexico require that a foreign-owned trademark be accompanied by a domestic-owned trademark, so that the brand identification will "rub off." Other countries, such as Taiwan, simply do not recognize copyright protection. Still other countries, such as the United States, limit copyright protection to encourage the domestic manufacture of books.

Marking requirements can be so burdensome that they effectively bar imports (for example, requiring marks of origin on small items, such as bolts, that are customarily sold in bulk quantities). Customs officials can be either lax or strict in guarding against bogus marks. They can overlook the entry of counterfeit goods or, conversely, they can impede the entry of legitimate goods.

GATT INITIATIVES

The GATT can be an effective forum for dealing with the enforcement aspect of intellectual property issues when goods cross national borders. It cannot be a substitute for existing organizations such as WIPO. The GATT Secretariat does not have, nor should it be given, the competence to arbitrate the complex technical and legal issues at play.

GATT rules could facilitate the freer flow of goods and services by establishing customs guidelines and minimum enforcement criteria. Two proposals deserve priority in the GATT context: (1) the establishment of a joint GATT-WIPO working party to develop guidelines for patent and trademark protection for high technology products, and (2) a renewal of efforts to negotiate a counterfeiting code, with participation by Asian newly industrializing countries (NICs) as part of their reciprocal concessions for OECD area trade liberalization.

The joint GATT-WIPO working party should focus on national regulations on intellectual property that distort trade and investment flows. For example, guidelines could be developed to ensure that compulsory licensing is narrowly limited to cases of patent abuse, that the resulting royalties are reasonable, and that compulsory licensing does not become a broad-scale substitute for import protection.

Efforts to negotiate a code of conduct on commercial counterfeiting (primarily to cover customs procedures for goods bearing bogus trademarks) have foundered since the Tokyo Round because of differences over appropriate customs procedures and penalties (forfeiture, for example), problems in enforcing such rights in national courts, and LDC concerns about disincentives to technology transfer. Trade in counterfeit goods seems to be growing, though no one has offered a believable ballpark estimate of the amount of counterfeit sales worldwide.

To answer the counterfeit threat, talks should be restarted promptly on a conditional MFN code that would give firms in each signatory country access to the other signatory's enforcement mechanisms. The mechanisms could then be used for the exclusion of counterfeit third-country goods. Moreover, each country would commit itself to adopt minimum standards for copyright and trademark protection. Adoption and enforcement of minimum standards by the Asian NICs is especially important; their cooperation would be encouraged by OECD trade liberalization in other areas.

Tariffs

It is fashionable to say that tariffs are no longer an important trade barrier and thus should not be a central focus in a new round. To be sure, *average* tariffs in developed countries are low. But high tariffs remain on particular goods, and additional high tariffs will emerge once QRs are converted to tariffs or auctioned quotas in the context of a new approach to adjustment. Moreover, tariff escalation remains a problem in OECD countries. Many developing countries, such as India and Mexico, still maintain extremely high *average* tariff barriers, accentuated by sharp peaks for particular sectors. Thus, contrary to conventional wisdom, tariffs should be an important part of the negotiating package.

TARIFFS AND ADJUSTMENT

"Born-again" tariffs and auctioned quotas could be an integral part of domestic adjustment programs and a new GATT safeguards system, as discussed earlier. The revenues derived from the new tariffs and auctioned quotas would be dedicated to financing adjustment programs for troubled industries.

Once QRs are converted into tariff equivalents (actual tariffs or auctioned quotas), the new levies should be subject to a negotiated schedule of liberalization. Tariff reductions (or liberalization of auctioned quotas) would be negotiated on a sector-by-sector basis to mesh with the adjustment needs of troubled industries, not according to a standard formula as in past rounds. These negotiations would have to deal with two problems: the problem of eliminating selectivity, when QRs that hit the trade of specific countries are transformed into MFN-tariffs or quota auctions that apply to all imports, and the risk that tariffs would be increased without a commensurate liberalization effort. GATT review of QR conversion and subsequent liberalization would help ensure the integrity of the entire process. This would follow a precedent set in the Tokyo Round, when the notoriously protective US American Selling

TABLE 3.2 **Average tariff rates in major OECD countries**

	United States	Japan	Canada	European Community
Finished manufactures	6.9	6.4	8.1	7.0
Semifinished manufactures	6.1	6.3	6.6	6.2
Raw materials	1.8	1.4	2.6	1.6

Source: Rudiger Dornbusch and Jeffrey A. Frankel, "Macroeconomics and Protection," University of Michigan, Conference on US Trade Policies in a Changing World Economy, Ann Arbor, Mich., 28–29 March 1985.

Price (ASP) system of tariff calculation for benzenoid chemicals and rubber footwear was converted to a normal valuation system with higher ad valorem rates, with agreement that the new rates would be lowered in a series of staged reductions.

Preferred suppliers under present selective quota arrangements would inescapably suffer losses under an MFN approach. These losses should be given appropriate credit in the context of overall trade negotiations. Moreover, if a country that substitutes auctioned quotas or tariffs for QRs does not adhere to the agreed liberalization schedule, it should pay compensation to its trading partners.

TARIFF ESCALATION

Most industrial countries apply lower import tariffs to commodities in raw form than to processed goods, and they tend to increase those rates with each successive level of processing. The tariff rates, for example, in the United States, Japan, and the European Community on rough logs are lower than those on wood pulp, which, in turn, are lower than those on paper and paper products. As shown in table 3.2, average tariffs for finished manufactures are about four times higher than those on raw materials in the major OECD countries.

The major purpose of tariff escalation schemes is to protect domestic processing industries against foreign competition, especially against countries with abundant resources in leather, ferrous and non-ferrous metals, foodstuffs, and wood products. The arithmetic of tariff escalation is straightforward. Suppose processing activities amount to 20 percent of value added. A 20 percent tariff on the processed item will raise prices by about 20 percent and thereby double the wages and profits of the processing industry. The net result of tariff escalation is to hinder the development and expansion of the processing capabilities of raw material countries, mainly LDCs, and to keep them as "hewers of wood and drawers of water."[48]

Just as developed countries try to protect their domestic processing capabilities by escalating tariffs, the developing countries try to encourage the development of their processing capabilities by taxing the export of primary products. The dimensions of a bargain are evident. In exchange for a rollback of high tariffs on processed goods by the developed countries, the LDCs (except the least developed countries) should reduce their export taxes on primary products. A 1979 study indicated that the simultaneous reduction of LDC export taxes on primary goods and OECD area tariffs on processed goods would expand LDC processing capabilities significantly with only a small contraction (less than 1 percent) in processing capabilities in the OECD area.[49]

Institutional Reforms

Countries may hesitate to work out new trading rules unless progress is also made to improve the enforcement of GATT provisions. Making the GATT work better would encourage greater national compliance with and political support for GATT provisions. For the GATT to function efficiently, three important institutional reforms need to be adopted: improving the dispute settlement system, strengthening the GATT Secretariat, and reinforcing ties with the International Monetary Fund (IMF) and the World Bank.

---

48. Between 1980 and the end of 1982, world commodity prices (excluding oil) fell by 35 percent to their lowest level in real terms in thirty years. Weak commodity prices give added urgency to dealing with tariff escalation problems. The unfavorable terms of trade movement means that processing activity is that much more attractive as a means of enhancing export growth.

49. Stephen S. Golub and J. M. Finger, "The Processing of Primary Commodities: Effects of Developed-Country Tariff Escalation and Developing-Country Export Taxes," *Journal of Political Economy*, vol. 87, no. 3, 1979. The analysis also predicts that a unilateral reduction in OECD area import tariffs would increase LDC processing by a greater amount but would also reduce OECD processing by more than 3 percent.

DISPUTE SETTLEMENT

The Tokyo Round made notable improvements in the procedures for resolving disputes. The most detailed rules were grafted onto the Subsidies Code: strict time limits were established for mediating disputes by neutral officials and for delivering conclusions by expert panels. Ironically, the Subsidies Code has been the focus of most dissatisfaction since 1980.

Dispute procedures work best when technical problems are at issue. When the problem is a political one, which means any problem involving substantial trade and employment interests, countries are more prone to ignore or to evade GATT rules than to change domestic programs and policies. The United States and the European Community have been the major culprits in unraveling the GATT dispute settlement system. The United States spent almost a decade fighting GATT condemnation of the export subsidies granted under the DISC program (the tax preference Domestic International Sales Corporation). In similar fashion, the European Community avoided complaints against its export programs for sugar and wheat flour. These dilatory habits were carried over to the new Subsidies Code.

The GATT cannot force sovereign states to change their policies to conform to GATT rules. Its power depends on a willingness by the major trading countries to take responsibility for maintaining the trading system and to refrain from unilateral actions that undercut the GATT.

Three reforms are needed. First, the GATT Secretariat should be empowered to notify new restrictive measures to the GATT Council. This procedure would enable affected third countries to seek redress through GATT dispute settlement procedures without the political onus of calling key trading partners to task. This would be particularly important in enforcing a ban on new voluntary restraint agreements.

Second, expert panels need to be reinforced. A major shortcoming of panels is that they are staffed by people who do not command the attention of trade officials in national capitals. What is needed is an internationally respected panel of elder statesmen to sit on all major cases.[50] The GATT already recognized the value of such an approach by commissioning a "Wisemen's" report on the overall problems facing the trading system. That

---

50. For an elaboration of this proposal, see Jeffrey J. Schott, "Can World Trade Be Governed?", *Challenge* (March/April 1982), pp. 47–48.

report calls for "a small permanent roster of nongovernment experts in GATT matters to examine disputes."[51] We would add one qualification: panelists should have sufficient political stature to ensure that their recommendations carry weight in the national decision-making processes.

Finally, disputes often arise over gray areas of the GATT that do not establish clear-cut obligations for GATT contracting parties (for example, agricultural export subsidies). Panels have been asked, in effect, to resolve problems that were left hanging in prior negotiations. Where ambiguities in GATT provisions cause disputes, panels will *not* be able to offer definitive findings; at best they can suggest approaches to clarify the rules.

To this end, panel findings should include questions of fact and law, *and* recommendations pertaining to GATT provisions that require interpretation or revision. Since revisions would alter the negotiated balance of concessions between contracting parties, countries should commit themselves to resolve contested disputes through negotiations. The GATT code committees provide an ideal locus for such continuing negotiations since they are comprised of the countries most interested in the particular provisions (subsidies or standards, for example) under dispute. If there is no appropriate code committee, the GATT Council should establish a special working party, open to all interested countries, as a negotiating forum.

THE GATT SECRETARIAT

The GATT was not designed to be an international *organization;* it emerged in the late 1940s as a second-best alternative to the stillborn International Trade Organization. This is reflected in the relatively small size of the secretariat (compared with the UNCTAD or OECD secretariats), which in turn constrains fresh analysis of trade issues.

The total GATT budget of $21 million (the US share was $3 million in 1984) is less than the *US* share of the budget of the International Labor Organization, the Food and Agriculture Organization, and many other bodies. The GATT budget could easily be doubled without significant consequences

---

51. Fritz Leutwiler, et al. *Trade Policies for a Better Future: Proposals for Action,* GATT, Independent Study Group (Geneva, March 1985), p. 46.

for national budgets.[52] The new resources should provide funding for a small number of additional staff members to monitor trade policies and adjustment programs, funding for panelists, and technical and legal support for the administration of new trade agreements.

COORDINATION WITH THE IMF AND WORLD BANK

The interrelationships of trade, money, and debt problems require close consultation betwccn the international institutions charged with responsibility for the maintenance of the global trade and financial system. While incorporated in the charters of the GATT, the IMF, and the World Bank, such consultations have generally been pro forma affairs with little impact on the decision-making process within each organization.

The Growth Round should focus increased attention on the importance of GATT coordination with the IMF and the World Bank. Finance ministers from industrial countries recognized the need for "the removal of trade-restricting practices and . . . the implementation of GATT recommendations and policies."[53] This will be particularly relevant with regard to trade liberalization in the LDCs and the differential phasing of liberalization schedules according to current account positions.

To serve this function, the GATT Secretariat should participate more actively in the preparation of IMF stabilization programs and in consideration of World Bank structural adjustment loans. This could take the form of GATT representation on staff missions and participation by a Deputy Director-General of GATT in appropriate IMF and World Bank deliberations. For this purpose, the GATT should establish a division for IMF and World Bank affairs.[54]

---

52. For example, a doubling of the GATT budget for staff expenditures over 1984 levels to meet the suggested added responsibilities would cost $14.7 million; the additional US share would be $2.1 million.

53. *Communiqué of the Ministers and Governors of the Group of Ten,* Tokyo, 21 June 1985, paragraph 54.

54. Other proposals for increased collaboration among multilateral institutions have been put forward by Miriam Camps and William Diebold, Jr. in *The New Multilateralism: Can the World Trading System be Saved?* (New York: Council on Foreign Relations, 1983).

Summary of the Package

Some may argue that our agenda for the Growth Round is far too ambitious: the negotiating package contains too many issues; several of those issues have escaped resolution for decades; and the overall package critically depends on a more buoyant world economy and complementary negotiations on the exchange rate system and LDC debt.

Our response to these misgivings is straightforward: negotiations must start with a broad agenda to satisfy the diverse interests of a large number of countries. A modest package will not keep the bicycle upright. Only a broad-based negotiation provides adequate scope for the kind of international horse trading that can overcome entrenched trade barriers.

The basic purpose of the Growth Round is to open export opportunities for competitive industries and to encourage adjustment in declining sectors. Resources can then be put to better use building new industries and jobs. The package has three parts: liberalizing traditional trade barriers, preempting new restrictions, and bolstering the GATT framework.

The seven strategic goals of the Growth Round detailed in chapter 2 find their practical implementation in the subject-by-subject recommendations of this chapter. A standstill on merchandise trade would start talks on the right foot, would halt the protectionist drift, and would demonstrate political resolve to tackle tough trade problems. To liberalize existing trade barriers, QRs should be converted to tariffs or auctioned quotas, followed by a negotiated reduction of restrictions. "Retariffication" simplifies, but does not substitute, for adjustment of industries down to a viable core. To ease the burden of adjustment, tariff and quota auction revenues should be dedicated to adjustment assistance programs.

Where protection has been particularly pervasive, as in agriculture and textiles, a very gradual approach is needed: liberalization would apply at first only to the marginal production that meets growth in demand. For agriculture, this translates into a cap on the amount of farm output eligible for existing government programs. For textiles, it means the renewal and then the gradual retirement of the MFA system.

Proposals on services, investment, and intellectual property seek to broaden the coverage of GATT principles to reach a larger share of world trade. These are areas where restrictions such as limited access to value-added networks, performance requirements, and patent and trademark infringements substantially distort trade. GATT rules are needed to ensure market access, rights of establishment, and the protection of intellectual property.

Action is also needed on "fairness" issues. Reforms of the Subsidies Code would strengthen discipline on agricultural export and mixed-credit subsidies, clarify permissible domestic subsidies, and provide needed enforcement against subsidies that distort competition in third-country markets. A commercial counterfeiting code would help staunch the flow of pirated goods and technologies. Negotiations on specific goods and services would relieve the "unfairness" problems created by tariff escalation and extravagantly unbalanced concessions.

Four tactics are proposed to accomplish these multiple tasks: the use of self-financed adjustment programs; the use of a conditional MFN approach for liberalizing and disciplining nontariff measures; the use of "snapback" provisions as a last resort when other countries do not fulfill their part of the bargain; and the phasing of concessions so that surplus countries accelerate implementation of their commitments.

Self-financed adjustment programs would enable inefficient industries and agriculture to downsize to a viable core. Conditional MFN would encourage erstwhile "free-riders" and "foot-draggers" to participate actively in developing new trade rules. To preserve the unity of the world trading system, however, the conditional MFN approach would not apply to tariff negotiations. "Snapback" provisions would enable countries to make concessions in one area prior to liberalization in other areas of interest to them. Moreover, the threat of a snapback would act as a prod to continuing negotiations. Phasing concessions would provide for accelerated liberalization by trade surplus countries like Japan; this in turn would benefit other countries and encourage their participation in new agreements.

Who are the winners and losers in grand multilateral negotiations? Clearly, all countries would gain from reinvigoration of the GATT trading system, a cornerstone of postwar prosperity; in addition, all countries would benefit from new growth opportunities provided by enhanced access to foreign markets.

The United States would be a winner. The tilt in the playing field would be righted by improving subsidy rules; by devising new GATT disciplines on trade in services, investment, and intellectual property; by rationalizing agricultural protectionism; and by enlarging the trade concessions made by Japan and the NICs. In exchange for these gains, the United States would have to make its own concessions, for example, by limiting support programs for agriculture and protection for steel, and textiles and apparel. But new adjustment measures, complemented by temporary protection under a new Safeguards Code, would substantially ease the burdens imposed on declining industries.

The European Community would be a winner. Agricultural reforms would free resources to spur new investment and employment in resource-starved high technology industries. Global liberalization would open export opportunities for both goods and services trade, particularly in East Asian NICs and in Japan. Multilateral talks would also serve as a catalyst for agreement on internal reforms (for example, to harmonize policies on services and telecommunications standards) and thereby encourage greater integration of the European market. These gains would come in return for European liberalization of barriers to agriculture; manufactures such as steel, textiles and apparel, and consumer electronics; and services such as insurance, banking, and data processing.

Japan would be a winner. The GATT system would prosper, and Japan would maintain relatively unfettered access to key markets. Indeed, Japan, along with the LDCs, would be a major beneficiary of a new Safeguards Code that put a stop to "voluntary" restraint agreements. To be sure, Japan would have to make substantial concessions, including major reductions in nontariff barriers to imports of goods and services—especially entrenched agricultural QRs and controls on high technology products.

Developing countries would be winners. LDCs have the most to gain from stronger GATT discipline over world trade. New safeguards rules and adjustment programs in the OECD area would promote LDC exports of a wide range of manufactured goods. In conjunction with increased capital flows from the IMF and the World Bank, new processing industries would flourish to take advantage of reduced tariff escalation in the OECD area. In return, the NICs would begin to dismantle the excessive apparatus of import protection that has hurt them more than it has hurt the world trading system. In particular, NICs would take three steps: first, convert their QRs into tariffs and bind those tariffs in the GATT; second, embark on the liberalization of services trade and performance requirements; and third, control commercial counterfeiting.

Finally, smaller OECD countries such as Canada, the Nordics, Switzerland, and Australia would be winners. Liberalization and adjustment programs in the United States and in the European Community would provide more secure access to their main export markets. Their efficient agricultural and high technology sectors would correspondingly gain. In turn, these countries would make concessions on hot-house manufactures, such as automobiles, steel, and textiles and apparel; on selected agricultural products; and on a wide range of services.

The "losers" are not countries, but industries that have already lost their ability to compete. These industries have survived through generous protection, at great expense to taxpayers and consumers in their home countries. New adjustment policies would help declining industries pare down to fighting weight. These industries may not be overjoyed at the prospect of trade negotiations, but their concerns should not dominate the proceedings. Trade negotiations are not a zero-sum game; "winners" far outnumber "losers" because liberalization encourages more efficient production, which means higher growth and more jobs. That, in short, is the key objective of a new trade round.

4   Launching a New Trade Round

In July 1978, when the economic summit leaders first met in Bonn, they "agreed on a comprehensive strategy covering growth, employment and inflation, international monetary policy, energy, trade and other issues of particular interest to developing countries."[1] In 1978, the leaders committed their respective countries to a series of complementary actions to foster growth throughout the world economy: each government except the United States agreed to a target level of economic growth, and the United States undertook commitments on energy pricing and filling the strategic petroleum reserve.

The Bonn Summit leaders in May 1985 faced many of the same growth and employment problems that plagued their precedessors seven years earlier. Unlike their precedessors, the summit leaders in 1985 did not agree on coordinated international initiatives to deal with global economic problems. Instead, they recommitted their governments to maintain existing policies on growth, employment, and trade.

Prospects for new General Agreement on Tariffs and Trade (GATT) talks were the focus of attention at the recent Bonn Summit, with the United States seeking agreement on a specific date for the start of negotiations. In order to forestall backsliding into protectionism or delays due to domestic political pressures, six of the seven leaders agreed on a 1986 starting date. Because of French opposition, however, no consensus was reached. The summit declaration merely echoed the conclusions of the Organization for Economic Cooperation and Development (OECD) ministers in April 1985 that "a new GATT round should begin as soon as possible" and added "[m]ost of us think that this should be in 1986."[2] Along with the impasse

---

1. *New York Times*, 18 July 1978, p. D12.

2. *Washington Post*, 5 May 1985, p. A30.

86

on trade, no new initiatives were taken on international monetary issues, such as the International Monetary Conference broached by US Treasury Secretary James A. Baker III during the April 1985 OECD meetings.

The summit inaction means that preparatory talks for a new round will proceed, but at a somewhat leisurely pace. The French will continue to block agreement within the European Community on a common negotiating position on agriculture at least until after French parliamentary elections in 1986; this in turn will complicate EC efforts to agree on an overall negotiating agenda. The LDCs, in turn, will hesitate to participate until they see both a greater commitment by the United States and Europe to deal with sensitive issues like agriculture and textiles, and an elaboration of how a negotiation on services would be conducted.

The Next Steps

The failure of the summit leaders to accelerate preparations for new trade talks represents a challenge, but not an insurmountable obstacle, to launching the Growth Round. The consensus-building process will be more trying without the pressure of a deadline for starting negotiations: the momentum for a new round has slowed; and many countries, including the United States, will have a harder time deflecting protectionist pressures. The following sections describe what needs to be done to move talks forward in the coming months.

BUILDING A CONSENSUS

Many developing countries are wary of embarking on a new round when so much remains to implement the Tokyo Round accords. Some LDCs have challenged the United States, Europe, and Japan to live up to their existing GATT commitments on vital issues such as textiles, apparel, and steel trade.

Recognizing these concerns, OECD ministers agreed in April 1985 to hold a meeting in the GATT "before the end of the summer to reach a broad consensus on subject matter and modalities" for a new trade round. The objective of the GATT meeting is to integrate the LDCs into the planning process for a new round to ensure the "active participation of a significant

number of . . . developing countries'' in the prospective negotiations.[3]
Extensive meetings are scheduled in the second half of 1985, culminating in
the November meeting of GATT contracting parties, to lay the groundwork
for further negotiations.

The negotiating agenda that emerges from these meetings must be broad
based to attract the varied trade interests of developed and developing
countries. Despite the summit impasse, agriculture is unlikely to be excluded
from the negotiations. The EC position announced in March 1985, which
the French extolled in Bonn, accepts new negotiations on agriculture ''within
the existing framework of the rules and disciplines in GATT,'' which the
European Community takes to exclude any question about ''the fundamental
objectives and mechanisms'' of the CAP.[4] What this really means is that the
European Community is willing to put agriculture on the negotiating table,
but has not yet decided what it wants to achieve in multilateral talks.

In addition, many countries may seek ''standstill'' commitments from the
United States, Europe, and Japan as a show of good faith in their pursuit of
trade liberalization. For example, the Development Committee of the International Monetary Fund (IMF) and World Bank in its April 1985 meeting
''called on governments to resist protectionism and, to the extent feasible,
roll back existing barriers to trade.''[5]

Some countries, particularly those in the European Community and many
LDCs, resist launching new negotiations until all countries have adequately
prepared. No one can argue with the merits of preparation, but the overtones
of the argument are disturbing. First, most of the key issues have been
around for a long time; the fact that the problems in textiles, agriculture, and
subsidies (to name just a few) have not been resolved does not reflect poor
preparation. Second, the newer issues, such as services and commercial
counterfeiting, also have been discussed in the GATT for several years,
although with less intensity than the more familiar issues. If countries have

---

3. OECD Ministerial Communiqué, 12 April 1985, paragraph 11.

4. Declaration by the EC Council of Ministers, 19 March 1985, paragraph 4.

5. Development Committee of the IMF and World Bank, *Press Communiqué*, 19 April 1985,
paragraph 6.

not prepared adequately, it is because their bureaucratic minds have not been "concentrated" by the prospect of negotiations.[6]

THE NEGOTIATING AGENDA

In the coming months, GATT members will engage in serious discussions on the prospective agenda for new trade talks. What the contracting parties need to decide is not the complete agenda for new trade talks, but the priority issues. One seemingly simple approach would entail adopting the current GATT work program as the priority agenda. This program was approved by ministers in 1982; it could now be said that preparations have been completed and that the results argue for new negotiations. However, several issues, notably services, investment, and high technology, received short shrift in 1982. Amending the GATT work program to include these issues could provoke a rancorous debate that would undermine the benefits of a quick-and-easy approach.

A better alternative would call for GATT members to agree on a statement of principles to guide the new multilateral round. Such a statement could include a standstill commitment on new barriers to merchandise trade (as detailed in chapter 2); a pledge to deal effectively with exchange rate and debt problems through bilateral and multilateral channels; and a commitment to reinforce GATT notification, consultation, and dispute settlement procedures. In addition, countries would recognize that the agenda would be open-ended and that all issues would be on the negotiating table. Groups of countries could then petition the GATT Secretariat to organize negotiating groups on various issues of interest to them, with participation open to all GATT members. This open-ended approach would sidestep a tedious battle to reach a consensus agenda and instead permit priorities to be set by the intensity of interest.

CONTINUING NEGOTIATIONS

Should the negotiations be organized and conducted as in past rounds with a single conclusion embodying many separate agreements? Or should the

---

6. Samuel Johnson's aphorism makes the point: "When a man knows he is to be hanged in a fortnight, it concentrates his mind wonderfully."

talks be conducted on a rolling agenda, punctuated from time to time by subject matter or country agreements?

Since the late 1940s, seven rounds of multilateral trade negotiations have been conducted under GATT auspices. In these rounds, bargains were finally agreed in one fell swoop, the benefits were available to all GATT members, and all parties implemented their tariff concessions at more or less the same rate. Thanks to the unconditional most-favored-nation (MFN) clause, this approach preserved the "unity" of the GATT trading partners. Further, it enabled each country to avoid identifying particular concessions given with concessions received, which in turn enabled the bargain to be sold as a package. Each country realized benefits according to approximately the same schedule. Clearly the "big bang" conclusion had many advantages.

By contrast, a rolling agenda approach to trade negotiations, implemented on a conditional MFN basis, would have two attractions. First, the traditional approach risks losing all if certain key problems cannot be resolved. In fact, the Tokyo Round came close to failure before final agreement was reached on the Subsidies Code.

Second, if the round lasts a number of years before tangible progress is made, patience may give out. Political support for trade talks requires more immediate gratification. The bicycle theory of negotiations works best if a series of key milestones are passed along the way.

To be sure, a rolling agenda of continuing negotiations raises legitimate concerns. It may be hard to sell concessions on certain issues to national legislatures when the resolution of other issues remains a mere gleam in the eye. This concern could be addressed with implementing legislation that contained snapback provisions. Concessions would be implemented as long as parallel progress was made in other areas. If progress stopped, the initial concessions would be withdrawn and the whole negotiation would unravel. The initial concessions would demonstrate that trade liberalization could proceed, while the threat of snapback action could serve as a prod for further bargaining.

The first issues concluded in a rolling agenda approach would depend on the political imperatives of the day. Some issues, such as services, clearly have a long fuse. Textiles, on the other hand, will have to be dealt with promptly because of the Multi-Fiber Arrangement (MFA) deadline (even if it is extended as recommended in chapter 3). The important point is to give the process credibility by periodic progress.

To that end, initial talks should focus on areas ripe for resolution. Along with a standstill on merchandise trade, the first priorities could include agreements on mixed-credit subsidies, a commercial counterfeiting code, selective tariff cuts (for example, to mitigate tariff escalation problems), and expanded dispute settlement provisions. Resolution of these problems could spur progress on more complicated issues such as agriculture, MFA reform, adjustment commitments, and a new safeguards code. Meanwhile, talks could proceed on issues with a longer time perspective, such as services and investment.

Negotiations based on a rolling agenda would have to be closely monitored and directed. To this end, progress reports should be issued every year to summit leaders, who could then agree on what issues deserved priority in the coming period and what new issues, if any, should be added to the priority agenda. For this purpose, the summit leaders should meet regularly with key leaders of developing countries—perhaps a triennial North-South summit—to coordinate the leadership of the trade talks.

Just below the summit, and meeting prior to the summit, would be the GATT Ministerial-level body proposed in the "Wisemen's" report.[7] This group would resemble the ad hoc group of ministers organized by former US Trade Representative William E. Brock that has met every few months since 1984 to discuss pressing trade issues.

The trade ministers would seldom have sufficient political clout to decide how and when to conclude talks on some issues while other matters remain on the negotiating table. Such decisions are weighty political calls that would ordinarily be taken by heads of state. However, the GATT Ministerial-level group could frame the issues for resolution at the summit.

Negotiating Alternatives

The GATT will reach a watershed in the second half of 1985: countries will either agree on a priority agenda for a multilateral round of trade negotiations to begin in 1986, or basic disagreements will lead the major trading nations to consider other means to achieve their trade objectives. The United States,

---

7. Fritz Leutwiler, et. al., *Trade Policies for a Better Future: Proposals for Action*, GATT, Independent Study Group (Geneva, March 1985), p. 48. The report suggested "establishment of a standing GATT Ministerial-level body of limited membership, but representative, through a constituency system, of all member countries."

in particular, has suggested two negotiating alternatives if GATT talks do not get underway.

Under this approach, the United States would open bilateral and plurilateral talks with interested countries on various topics, using different forums as appropriate. Talks could focus on the reduction of specific trade barriers (for example, restrictive standards for high technology products) or the development of new trade rules (for example, a commercial counterfeiting code). In most instances, concessions would be accorded on a conditional MFN basis, despite possible conflicts with GATT Article I. At an advanced stage, the "à la carte" approach could involve free trade area agreements consistent with GATT Article XXIV; the Caribbean Basin Initiative and recent overtures to Canada are examples of how liberalization could proceed prior to or in the absence of multilateral negotiations.

The "à la carte" approach could get talks started among countries that have the most to gain, namely the countries that are likely to form the core groupings for new agreements, while leaving the door open for participation by other countries. It might eventually generate enough negotiating momentum for the individual talks to "fuse" into a multilateral round. It is a risky approach, however. A series of bilateral and minilateral initiatives could badly weaken the remaining fabric of the multilateral trading system designed in Havana 40 years ago.

THE FREE TRADE AREA APPROACH

The history of postwar trade policy is punctuated by free trade areas (FTAs), including the European Community itself; the widening of the European Community to include Greece, Spain, and Portugal; the European Free Trade Association (EFTA); the Australia–New Zealand closer economic agreement; and, most recently, the FTA between the United States and Israel. FTAs have also been worked out on a sectoral basis, for example, the US-Canadian auto pact and, for "non-sensitive" products, the Caribbean Basin Initiative.

FTAs could represent a catchy approach for boosting the liberal side of the trade agenda, providing a useful foil against protectionist pressures. Talks with an FTA flavor are underway or under active consideration between the European Community and the EFTA; the United States and Canada; and the United States, Australia, and New Zealand. FTAs are consistent with GATT as long as the conditions of Article XXIV are met, notably, the elimination of customs duties and other border barriers on "substantially all the trade" between the partners "within a reasonable length of time." Conceivably, a series of FTAs could serve as building blocks for a wider industrial free trade area with negotiations toward that goal opening in the year 2000.

RISKS AND OPPORTUNITIES

Both the "à la carte" approach and the free trade area approach have their risks. While the prospects of trade liberalization emanating from bilateral or plurilateral negotiations are tempting, especially if multilateral talks are foundering, several negative developments could follow from "minilateral" deals.

The GATT "Wisemen" argued that the past use and abuse of Article XXIV in permitting FTAs "set a dangerous precedent for further special deals, fragmentation of the trading system, and damage to the trade interests of non-participants."[8] Although FTAs and sectoral arrangements may expand trade among the countries involved, they lessen interest of those countries in improving the global trading system. Size alone makes a difference. For example, the European Community has found it increasingly difficult to liberalize its external trade restrictions as the number of member countries has grown, for the simple reason that more and more interest groups have to be accommodated.

Further, there is an important political aspect. Bilateral deals run the risk that economic concessions will be tied to political concessions, with a loss of economic efficiency and an attendant increase in diplomatic ill-will. The prewar history of bilateral trading arrangements and the postwar history of tied aid and trade credits are replete with such problems.

Nonetheless, the process of minilateral agreements is likely to continue for many years to come. The pioneer in this process is the European Community, which in 1986 will add Spain and Portugal to reach 12 countries. Internal EC trade now accounts for 21 percent of all trade among GATT

---

8. Leutwiler, et al. *Trade Policies for a Better Future*, p. 41.

members. In addition, the European Community has concluded bilateral trade agreements with all countries bordering the Mediterranean except Libya, and with 66 Caribbean, African, and Pacific nations under the Lome Aid and Trade Pact. At the same time, the European Community and the EFTA are removing barriers to intra-European trade, especially in high technology trade and government procurement.

The United States also is continuing to solidify trade and investment ties with its neighbors and political allies. The US-Canadian auto pact in 1965 was a key step in this direction. More recently, the United States concluded the Caribbean Basin Initiative (1983), a bilateral agreement with Mexico on subsidies and countervailing duties (1985), and a free trade area agreement with Israel (1985). Talks will soon begin on a bilateral trade and investment pact with Mexico, and perhaps on a comprehensive free trade arrangement with Canada, including such sectors as computer services, petrochemicals, and subway cars. Free trade area talks between the United States, Australia, and New Zealand are not impossible.[9]

We draw two conclusions from the drift of events. First, a genuine multilateral round offers the best approach for improving the world trading system and the welfare of all GATT members. An ambitious negotiation is more likely to generate forward momentum than narrowly targeted talks. Such a negotiation should interest a far wider circle of countries (including the newly industrializing countries, NICs) and generate sufficient political enthusiasm in Brussels, Tokyo, and Washington to put trade matters closer to the top of the agenda. Second, if a multilateral round stalls, minilateral agreements are not a bad alternative for enlivening the liberalization process. But it is critically important that minilateral agreements be open to new members, and that the agreements be viewed as building blocks for a larger GATT free trade area, not as an end in themselves.

Conclusion: Trading for Growth

Few countries are content with the way the world trading system now operates. Rules are vague and weakly enforced. Trade protection has

---

9. Concerning this approach, Clayton Yeutter, the new US Trade Representative, argues that FTAs should not be considered "mutually exclusive" of broader GATT talks. He adds the United States will not enter such agreements "unless they mesh" with global talks. See *Wall Street Journal*, 9 July 1985, p. 33.

increased, prompting imitation or retaliation. Massive trade and current account imbalances threaten a further upward-ratcheting of protection. Most important, exchange rate misalignments severely distort trade flows and threaten to reignite the LDC debt crisis. No one doubts the seriousness of these problems. If they continue, they will erode the trading system and undermine economic growth in developed and developing countries alike.

While trade negotiations are not a panacea for ills of the world economy, neither are they a placebo. In conjunction with appropriate monetary and fiscal policies, trade reforms can contribute to economic growth and employment. Trade negotiations can halt the drift toward protectionism and restore momentum for liberalization.

However, trade reforms take time to be negotiated, much less implemented. It will be years before governments have to face the hard political decision to liberalize entrenched barriers; hopefully by then, the economic climate will be much improved. This contingency adds urgency to the parallel tasks of resolving the problems of exchange rate misalignments and LDC debt.

Trade negotiations hold the risk of import competition and the attraction of export opportunities. Each country must weigh the costs and benefits of liberalization against the consequences of inaction or a further drift to protection. In this light, we think the case for new trade negotiations becomes compelling.

This study has set forth reasons why negotiations are needed and has proposed strategies for them to succeed. It has explored the objectives of the major trading countries, the issues that need to be addressed, and possible approaches for pursuing negotiations. Some of the ideas represent conventional wisdom, some revive schemes raised in prior rounds, and some offer provocative new thoughts. Most important is the strategy for combining the old with the new to reach rewarding trade-offs between issues, sectors, and countries.

We have provided a road map, not a negotiating manual, to help countries choose the most appropriate course for their economic growth and development. We believe trade negotiations can play an important part.

Appendix   The Contribution of Trade to Growth: A Rough Calculation

How large is the supply-side contribution that rapid trade growth makes to faster economic growth on a global basis? This is an important question, but it is also a difficult question, and one that has received surprisingly little attention. To be sure, many scholars have examined the consequences of liberal trade policies for particular countries, especially the successful Asian newly industrializing countries (NICs), but few scholars have analyzed the global growth consequences of larger trade. This appendix is designed more to prompt needed scholarship than to provide definitive answers.

If we assume that, in the 1980s, a $10 billion expansion in imports of goods and services will on average free resources that directly and indirectly can produce an additional $12.5 billion of goods and services, a very rough guess can be attempted as to the supply-side contribution of larger trade to global growth. The $12.5 billion figure reflects a conservative estimate that tariff and nontariff barriers in the world economy today average some 15 percent and that, in addition, export sectors in each country average 10 percent greater productivity than import-competing sectors.[1] In earlier postwar years, $10 billion of import expansion probably enabled much more than $12.5 billion of additional production, because trade barriers were higher.[2]

---

1. Based on estimates in chapter 5 of Gary Clyde Hufbauer and Howard F. Rosen, *Trade Policy for Troubled Industries*, POLICY ANALYSES FOR INTERNATIONAL ECONOMICS (Washington: Institute for International Economics, forthcoming 1985), the tariff equivalent of US import protection (tariff and nontariff barriers) was about 10 percent in 1985. Other important trading regions probably exhibit somewhat higher rates of protection. Frictions within national economies would seem to ensure that export sectors are at least 10 percent more productive than import-competing sectors.

2. The Kennedy Round cut industrial country tariffs on dutiable goods by about 60 percent. The Tokyo Round cut another 26 percent. As a result, average industrial country tariffs, including duty-free goods, have dropped from about 11 percent in 1965 to about 5 percent in 1985. In

T A B L E A-1   **Estimated contribution of world trade growth to potential growth of world output (percentage)**

	Growth of world output	Growth of world trade	World trade as percentage of world output[a]	Contribution of world trade growth to potential world output[b]	Share of world output growth made possible by trade growth[c]
1953–63	4.3	6.1	7.7	0.22	5.1
1963–73	5.1	8.9	8.7	0.27	5.3
1973–83	2.5	2.8	15.8	0.11	4.4

Source: IMF, *International Financial Statistics: Yearbook 1982*, vol. 35, pp. 66–75, and *Yearbook 1984*, vol. 37, pp. 104–17, 120–23. GATT, *International Trade,* various issues; Irving Kravis, Alan Heston, and Robert Summers, *World Product and Income: International Comparisons of Real Gross Product* (Baltimore, Md.: The Johns Hopkins University Press, 1982), p. 344.

a. The figures refer to 1960, 1970, and 1980 respectively.

b. This calculation is based on the following framework:

dT = annual growth in trade, expressed in constant dollars;

W = world economic output, expressed in constant dollars;

$\frac{(x)\,(dT)}{W}$ = assumed contribution that trade growth makes to potential world output, expressed as a percentage of world output. For the decade 1953–63, x is set equal to 0.50; for the decade 1963–73, x is set equal to 0.35; for the decade 1973–83, x is set equal to 0.25;

$\frac{(x)\,(dT)}{W} = (x)\,(dT/T)\,(T/W)$

contribution of trade growth to potential output equals the product of: x, times the growth rate of trade, times trade as a fraction of output.

c. Calculated as: contribution of world trade growth to potential world output divided by growth of world output.

Rough guesses based on these assumptions suggest that the expansion of world trade in the last decade added at least 0.11 percent annually to world growth potential (table A-1). For many countries, especially the Asian NICs which practice export-led growth strategies, and debt-ridden Latin American

addition, quantitative restraints imposed for balance of payments reasons by Japan and Europe were greatly liberalized in the 1950s and 1960s. See UNCTAD, *The Kennedy Round Estimated Effects on Tariff Barriers* (Geneva, 1968), especially pt. 2, "The Structure of Protection in Industrial Countries and its Effect on the Exports of Processed Goods from Developing Countries"; and Alan V. Deardorff and Robert M. Stern, "Economic Effects of the Tokyo Round," *Southern Economic Journal,* vol. 49 (January 1983).

countries that face severe balance of payments constraints, trade makes an even greater contribution to GNP growth.

In any event, on a global basis in a world with nearly $9 trillion of output in the market economy countries,[3] a figure as small as 0.11 percent amounts to $9 billion per year. In a good year like 1984, when the volume of trade grew by 9 percent, the addition to world growth potential might exceed 0.30 percent, or about $27 billion. Since the contribution of trade to growth operates in a cumulative fashion, the growth of trade over a period of 10 years may well have added 1 percent to potential world output, about $90 billion in 1984.

In the early postwar years, a $10 billion expansion of global imports might well have freed resources that, on average, could directly and indirectly produce an additional $15 billion of goods and services. In the 1950s and early 1960s, it is not implausible to suppose that tariff and nontariff barriers averaged 30 percent, and that export sectors were at least 20 percent more productive than import-competing sectors.

These admittedly rough parameters suggest that the expansion of world trade may have added at least 0.20 percent annually to world growth potential in the early postwar period. All in all, the share of world GNP growth made possible by trade expansion in the postwar period could have been 4 percent to 5 percent (see table A-1).

---

3. Extrapolated from Kravis, Heston, and Summers, *World Product and Income*, p. 344.